0140

~~Donald E. Dickson~~ on

STANDING FAST

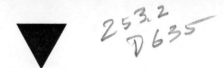

Mastering Ministry's Pressure Points

STANDING FAST

Ministry in an Unfriendly World

ED DOBSON
WAYNE GORDON
LOUIS MCBURNEY

MULTNOMAH BOOKS

STANDING FAST
© 1994 by Christianity Today, Inc.

Published by Multnomah Books
Questar Publishers, Inc.
Sisters, Oregon

Printed in the United States of America

International Standard Book Number: 0-88070-646-5

Most Scripture quotations are from the *New International Version* (©1973, 1978, 1984
by the International Bible Society; used by permission of Zondervan Publishing House).

94 95 96 97 98 99 00 01 — 10 9 8 7 6 5 4 3 2 1

Contents

Introduction

Life on an alien planet is usually unpleasant.

I've seen what happened to Captain Kirk when he materialized on far-off planets in *Star Trek*. Sometimes landing parties from the starship *Enterprise* faced poisonous atmosphere, other times killer plants or mutants with death rays. On other planets still, Kirk and Spock survived meteor showers, warrior races from another time, assassin robots, or deadly radiation. Alien planets are no place to vacation, much less pastor a church.

Sadly, good old planet Earth feels more and more like an alien planet to many Christians and church leaders. We face one threat after another, from hostile zoning boards to the secular press, from the warped images people have of churches and ministers to daily perversions of biblical morality.

Though we pastors preach about not letting the world squeeze us into its mold, we find it difficult not to succumb. This pressure affects not only our ministries but also our families.

For example, after pastoring in a lower middle-class neighborhood in Chicago, in 1987 I moved with my family to pastor a church in Arlington Heights, Illinois, an upper middle-class Chicago suburb. We enrolled our two junior-high boys in the public school. They felt the change immediately. They had come from a Christian school where some children felt fortunate to have a decent shirt; now they were at an upscale public school where they were judged by the names on their sneakers.

Within two weeks, my boys came home insisting they needed new pants and shoes, with the right labels. I said their clothes looked fine. They said other kids made fun of them. I proceeded to appeal to Scripture, common sense, and traditional American values, and finally I pleaded for mercy on my pocketbook. But the ponderous weight of my arguments had no effect.

I got pretty upset. I was angry at our materialistic culture and the well-off teenagers who judged people solely by how they looked. I was angry that these teens so quickly foisted their values on my children. In the end, however, we bought the clothes my boys needed to avoid being misfits.

Living in an alien culture forces tough choices on pastors: How much do we insist our families live against the grain, as we so often preach? How much do we bend the church to the culture to attract people? Where do we get the resources to continue to minister in a culture that has little respect for the ministry?

The questions of how to live and minister in the world without being of the world can't be answered with a one-two-three formula. The three authors of this book — Ed Dobson, Wayne Gordon, and Louis McBurney — know that. They don't offer easy answers, but they have faced the tough situations and learned from them.

Ed Dobson

As we sat in his office, the first thing I noticed in conversation with Ed Dobson is he says what's necessary and then stops. No excess words. No excess sentences. Always clear, grammatically correct, and laconically to the point. He goes instinctively to the pith of any issue.

A man in such control of his words is also in control of himself and his province. But Ed Dobson is not a control nut. In fact one thing he says he has learned about pastoring a large church is it is beyond control. He leads Calvary Church by setting an example, preaching truth, giving initiative, but Ed Dobson cannot control his church — a realization with which he seems completely content.

If Ed were overly worried about keeping the large Calvary Church congregation under his thumb, he certainly wouldn't take so many risks. He has been at the helm of Calvary Church since 1988, but after only a few years he started a Saturday-night seekers service, where weekly he answers the most demanding questions anyone can fire his way. Saturday Night resulted from his passion to evangelize the unchurched.

That passion prompted another risky move. Convinced that the church needed to minister to those hurting the most, he led Calvary Church to reach out to homosexuals and those suffering from AIDS. Since then his church has become a high-profile example of how to help those dying of AIDS to find housing.

Ed also takes risks on Sunday morning. He is known for preaching systematically through the Bible and, in the process, tackling the controversial issues pastors prefer to avoid. He faces those issues with one overarching concern: to tell people what the Bible says, not what Ed Dobson thinks.

Also, when a well-known pastor failed morally, Ed got personally involved in his friend's restoration, even though he knew that stand would be unpopular with many.

Before coming to Calvary Church, Ed served as vice president at Liberty University in Lynchburg, Virginia, worked for Moral Majority, and appeared on dozens of TV and radio shows to discuss controversial issues.

Ed knows about taking a stand in an unfriendly world, yet he does so without being "in your face." He is a peacemaker with convictions, a bridge builder with a conscience, an even-tempered mover and shaker.

He earned a doctorate in higher education from the University of Virginia. He is author of *What the Bible Really Says about Marriage, Divorce, and Remarriage,* and *Starting a Seeker-Sensitive Service: How Traditional Churches Can Reach the Unchurched.* He is a consulting editor with LEADERSHIP.

Wayne Gordon

In preparation for this book, we spent several days with Wayne Gordon, pastor of Lawndale Community Church in Chicago, and got to eat at some of his favorite neighborhood restaurants. On our way to lunch one day, we worked our way through the church hallways, which are crowded every day of the week, and once outside walked southwest on Ogden Avenue, past the fresh pastel facade of his church, past the charred, gutted remains of a building across the street, past a Dumpster where old roofing was being thrown by workers atop the building (Lawndale Community Church had recently bought the building, and volunteers from Kansas were now remodeling it).

We walked by the Chicago Transit Authority bus garage — and the warm, burnt smell of diesel exhaust. Wayne, who has a boyish grin and mounds of joyful energy, greeted virtually every person on the sidewalk by name. They address him as "Coach," a remnant of his days as a teacher and football and wrestling coach at local Farragut High School.

At the intersection of Pulaski, Ogden, and Cermak, half a block from the church, we came to Rally's, a new fast-food restaurant. Wayne is proud of this burger place because it says something about the ministry of Lawndale Community Church. Where fifteen years ago no one would risk investing a dime in the Lawndale neighborhood — the fifteenth poorest community in the nation — now a chain had enough confidence to open a new franchise.

The area around Lawndale Community Church has become

an island of hope in the midst of decay. Neighborhood residents are well aware of Lawndale Community Church because it touches some 50,000 people a year through its free medical clinic, housing ministry (buying and remodeling abandoned buildings), recreation programs in a first-rate gym (a full-court gym with Plexiglass backboards!), Bible studies, leadership development, youth learning center, job-finding programs, and of course, church services attended by three hundred people each week.

The respect hasn't always been there. Wayne, a solidly built, former linebacker, is a white man in a black neighborhood. People at first didn't trust him; they questioned his motives. Wayne has been the victim of random crime more times than he now bothers to count. He has been criticized and opposed by government leaders, neighborhood groups, and angry neighbors. Wayne has learned how to minister in a tough setting.

Wayne is a graduate of Wheaton College and Northern Baptist Theological Seminary. In 1978, after teaching at Farragut High School in Chicago for three years, Wayne started Lawndale Community Church in Chicago. In 1992 Wayne changed his role at the church to outreach pastor as he led the church to take on an African-American shepherding pastor. He is president of the Christian Community Development Association, a nationwide group committed to the restoration of impoverished areas, and a contributing writer to *Urban Family* magazine.

Louis McBurney

Louis McBurney is a pastor's advocate.

One church board sent their pastor to Marble Retreat to work through the emotional aftershocks of serious conflict within the church. To know how he should approach the counseling, Louis called the board chairman and asked, "Does the church plan to terminate or support the pastor? Should I prepare him to work through a transition, or should I help him with conflict issues in the church?"

The board chairman assured Louis they did not plan any action on the pastor's employment for at least a year.

Two weeks after the pastor returned to work at the church, the board terminated him. After hearing the news, Louis phoned the board chairman and confronted him over the board's duplicity.

Louis counseled another pastor suffering emotional burnout. The church had loaded more expectations on the pastor than any human could bear. Louis wrote a letter to the church board, explaining burnout and how the board could help their pastor by easing their expectations.

Marble Retreat center reflects the advocate heart of Louis McBurney. He located his ministry to pastors among the ponderosa pines on the side of a Colorado mountain overlooking a peaceful valley because he knew hurting pastors need a refuge. What Marble Retreat offers to the eye and ear, Louis McBurney provides for the soul: a refuge. He is a natural care giver — gentle, compassionate, understanding — virtues he attributes both to the Holy Spirit and his mother's example.

At the same time, to sustain his ministry he has had to be as resilient as a tree on a winter mountainside. Following the call of God to leave mainstream psychiatric practice and start a ministry to pastors has been the most challenging thing Louis has ever done. He knows what financial pressure is all about, and he understands ministry in an unfriendly world. When secular psychologists at professional conferences ask what he does, Louis's reply — "I counsel clergy who are burned out or in crisis" — leaves them fumbling for something to say.

But any Texan who lives in Colorado is accustomed to going against the grain (Coloradans don't root for the Dallas Cowboys). Louis earned his M.D. degree from Baylor College of Medicine and served his internal medicine internship at Methodist Hospital in Houston and his psychiatric residency at Mayo Clinic. He is the founder of Marble Retreat, a counseling center for clergy, begun in 1974. He is the author of *Every Pastor Needs a Pastor, Families under Stress*, and *Counseling Christian Workers*. Louis is on numerous boards of directors and is a consulting editor for LEADERSHIP.

It has been said, "We are not at our best perched at the summit; we are climbers, at our best when the way is steep."

As our culture becomes increasingly alien and hostile, the work and the challenge of ministry steepens, but as the authors of this volume show, pastors truly are at their best when facing an unfriendly world.

— *Craig Brian Larson*
contributing editor, LEADERSHIP
Carol Stream, Illinois

PART ONE

Ministry in Modern Society

The secular world supports ministries that help people with their physical and mental needs, especially if the church tackles problems no one else can or will.

— Wayne Gordon

CHAPTER ONE

The Church Embattled

I am the founding pastor of Lawndale Community Church, located on the west side of Chicago in the fifteenth-poorest neighborhood in America. You might guess we've had our share of crises.

After meeting in a storefront for several years, we purchased a former factory. It had space adequate for offices, a worship center, classrooms, and community services such as a medical clinic and a gym, but it needed major renovation. In order to have a usable gym, for instance, we needed to excavate six feet of dirt from the basement.

We started with a few strong backs and some picks, shovels,

and wheelbarrows. In their spare time, people from our church, of all ages, wheeled one load of dirt after another into our adjoining lot. The pile steadily grew. After nine months, someone donated a bulldozer and driver; we knocked a hole in the side of the building to fit the bulldozer through, and in three days the job was done.

But what to do with that mountain of dirt? When we received our building permit, the city said we could use the dirt for berms around our lot. But we had a lot more dirt than we needed for that. So for over a year, the dirt sat there.

Then trouble struck. One night a man hid behind the dirt pile, jumped out, and mugged a passerby. A short time later, it happened again. One tragic night, someone from behind the dirt pile shot and killed a passerby. Then another person was shot and killed. We had been working to turn our inner-city street into a place of light and peace, but it had turned even darker.

Naturally, we became desperate to move the dirt. The lowest bid from an excavation company to haul it away was $20,000 — way out of our budget. We tried to give the dirt away; we advertised in trade journals for contractors looking for dirt. No response.

The heat went up when I received a phone call from our alderman saying he was coming to my office. He arrived with the president of the neighborhood block club. The block president quickly came to the point:

"It's your church's fault we're having so much violence here!" And his resentment had some racial overtones: "Here you are, a white guy thinking you can come in here and treat us with disrespect. You shouldn't be here!"

The alderman intervened. "Reverend, we need to get rid of this dirt."

I explained what we had tried to do and described our plans to use some of the dirt for the eight-foot-high berms.

"We don't want any berms!" the block president interrupted. "Gangs will hide behind them. There will be more muggings and shootings."

I felt embattled and defensive. We had been living and working in the neighborhood with good intentions, but some people didn't see that. All they saw was violence and tragedy as a result of our efforts. Racial tensions, it seemed, were not lowering but rising! And now the political establishment viewed us as a problem.

Though this episode was resolved (as you'll see), it revealed a common tension. No matter the church setting, hostility against the church is a growing phenomenon in our culture. Whether the source is the local zoning board, the judicial system, the media, or the next door neighbor, churches are having to learn to function in a culture that sometimes views them more as a detriment than a benefit.

Are those outside the church really as hostile as they seem? Is it possible to get them on our side? What should we do when faced with implacable, unmistakable opposition?

Keep It in Perspective

I've found that hostility against the church is rarely hostility against the church per se. A lot of it has nothing to do with our faith, and the sooner we put that into perspective, the better.

When I first tried to move into a black Chicago neighborhood, I went from apartment to apartment listed for rent. But for over a month, each landlord would say, "We don't have anything available." I didn't understand what the problem was.

One day I knocked on the door of a manager of a twenty-six-unit complex; I told her I wanted to see the three-room apartment for rent. The manager, Mrs. Washington, said, "We don't 'mix' in this building." It was my white skin that was the problem.

I persisted, and finally she showed me the apartment. A short time later, I moved in. Though neighbors were friendly enough, I felt they held me at a distance. They could not figure out why a white man would want to live in their neighborhood. I didn't blame them for their attitude, but I was troubled by it.

That December, after living in the neighborhood for four months, I flew home for Christmas, leaving my locked van parked in front of the apartment. When I returned a week later, I found the driver's side window of my van broken and my spare tire sitting on the front seat.

At the front door of my apartment, I met Mrs. Washington. "I'm so glad you're here," she said anxiously. Handing me a sheet of paper, she said, "Call the police and ask for this officer."

When the police arrived, they were shocked to find I was white.

"You live here?"

"Yes."

"This is your van?"

"Yes."

"This is unbelievable," the policeman said. "Within minutes of the break-in, three people on this street called us."

The person who had broken into my van was a heroin addict who lived two doors down from me. My black neighbors, who seemed to have been suspicious of me, had called the police on a life-long neighbor. Then, for the next twenty-four hours until I returned home, they set up a neighborhood watch to keep an eye on my van.

I was glad I hadn't let my false assumptions get the better of me. Furthermore, I began to see things from the landlord's point of view: There were virtually no white people in North Lawndale; many of these landlords probably suspected I was a drug dealer. I was a potential source of trouble. Why bother?

The same is true of some of the hostile reactions churches get from neighbors. Often their motives have nothing to do with our faith; they are just concerned about property values, flooding, and traffic congestion — things we're all concerned about in our own neighborhoods.

Sometimes, though, we in the church bring the opposition on ourselves.

After we bought our building in 1983, I went to a neighborhood block club meeting to communicate the vision of our church. During the meeting someone asked, "Why are you here?"

I stood up and said, "God has given me a supernatural love for black people. It's something spiritual, a calling from God on my life. I'm going to live out my life and faith in the black community."

Someone interrupted me, "Are you saying that in order to love black people, you need supernatural ability from God?"

"No, no. That's not what I'm saying," I replied.

"Are you saying our neighborhood needs you? That we can't make it unless a white man comes to save us?"

The night ended with hard feelings. I had been culturally insensitive and naive. I look back and realize the hostility that evening was brought on by me.

Finally, we need to see our problems with other people in the largest of perspectives. We may need to remind ourselves that even though we are God's special people, he's not necessarily going to treat us specially.

My first two years in the city, no one broke into my home. When I decided to marry, I planned to bring my wife with me to live in North Lawndale. Friends warned, "You can't do that. You can't bring your wife into that neighborhood. It's too rough." I thought otherwise: we were doing God's work, sacrificing a great deal to live there. Surely he would protect us.

The night we returned from our honeymoon, Anne and I found that our home had been broken into. We were devastated and hurt.

But that was only the beginning. Regularly for the years since we've been here, something troubling happens; my car has been stolen, broken into, and involved in accidents; burglars have broken into our home ten times.

After the tenth break-in, I was irate. "Why are you letting this happen, Lord?"

He communicated something clearly to my spirit. "Wayne, you think you're pretty great, don't you?"

"What do you mean, Lord?"

"You think you're better than the people around you. You have to understand I love the prostitute living next door to you as much as I love you. You have to quit expecting preferential treatment. If it rains in this neighborhood, it's going to rain on you. If it snows here, it's going to snow on you. Crime is a part of this community, so you're going to experience it, too."

Turning Outsiders into Your-siders

Our ministry regularly sends out a prayer letter. I sign it, "Yours for a better world through Christ, Wayne." A Jewish man, the CEO of a major corporation, receives that letter and responds each time by sending us a thousand dollars. He is not a messianic Jew.

Why does he support us? And why have so many secular agencies — government and private agencies that you would think would be hostile to us — worked with us? How have we turned potential critics into friends?

In addition to ministering to people's spirits, we minister to their bodies and minds — and most people, no matter their faith, can support those types of ministries.

● *Ministry to the body.* At Lawndale Community Church, we run a medical clinic with seventeen doctors and eleven nurses on staff. We have an office in the state welfare building. Previously, a pregnant woman on welfare had to wait up to six weeks before receiving funds for vitamins and prenatal checkups. Since the first six weeks of pregnancy are crucial to a child's health, we began a program providing care until the state funding kicks in.

We also have a housing development corporation that buys abandoned properties, remodels the buildings, and sells them to people in the church and neighborhood for affordable prices.

● *Ministry to the mind.* Many are alarmed and critical about what happens in our public schools, and rightfully so. But rather than run from the school system, we thought we should get involved.

Every year we host an appreciation dinner for all the teachers and staff of the three nearby public schools. We award plaques, for instance, for the most creative teacher of the year. Since the meeting is held at our church, we say a prayer and perhaps have special music with a Christian message, but I don't preach.

Also, when one school couldn't fund a program, we gave it

$500 to do so. And we let these local schools use our basketball court at no charge.

Who, then, do these schools pick for their graduation speaker or assemblies? Often they ask me or my co-pastor, Carey Casey. In a low-key way, we're able to talk about God and how he helps us in life.

And recently when the administrator of one of these schools was going through a tough time, he started attending our church services; he knew we cared.

The secular world supports ministries that help people with their mental and physical needs, especially if the church tackles problems no one else can or will.

The key steps to meeting those neglected needs are these:

1. Invite the church's neighbors to discuss neighborhood needs.

2. At the meeting, let them do the talking. Make a note of their suggestions (sidewalks need fixing; moms need a place to drop off their kids once a week; high schoolers need a place for activity; young couples need marriage counseling), no matter your first impression of its feasibility.

3. Determine with your church's leaders what items on the list are doable.

How much you can realistically accomplish isn't the issue. Church resources are limited, after all. But even a small start can communicate a big message: the church is there to help. That will get and keep neighbors on your side.

You Can Play By Your Rules

Some churches feel that if they are going to win the approval or support of the neighborhood and local social agencies, they have to alter significantly their ministry. We have not found this to be true. In fact, people respect our distinctives as a Christian church. Usually the only thing they ask for is something we would do anyway.

A secular charitable organization recently arranged a meeting with me and the pastors of two other churches to see if they could support us in some of our social work. They respected how we were getting the job done, and they wanted to funnel their money through a proven organization.

But that posed them some difficulties. "Our by-laws state that we cannot give our money to a church," they said. "But if you could completely separate your social work from your church, then we could give you some money."

"The bottom line," I answered, "is that without our church, our development corporation (which handles all our housing, education, and economic development) would be ineffective. Our Christian faith is the motive for all we do. The church has to remain in control of the development corporation."

They eventually decided they would bend the rules and give their money to an organization run by a church.

And contrary to what one might think, our health clinic is not required to have a particular abortion policy as a result. Our clinic does not perform abortions, nor does it counsel anyone to have an abortion or make referrals for abortion. Furthermore, this secular charity has not meddled with what I preach or with any policies of the church. They respect the fact that we are a church and have a unique mission.

They did, of course, have two conditions for working with us. But these did not pose a problem.

1. No discrimination. In our prenatal care program, we were required to help anyone, Asian or Hispanic, Muslim or Jew, who came for help. But this was our intent in the first place.

2. No manipulative proselytizing. Our medical care, they said, couldn't be dependent on people listening to a sermon or reading a piece of literature.

Again, that wasn't a concern, because we know our ministry will provide plenty of evangelistic opportunities without our initiating evangelistic conversations. We are not prohibited from talking about God or about our church with anyone. Our doctors can *ask* a patient if he or she would like to pray, but we cannot require a patient to pray.

Whether it's helping with funding or just respecting what we do, the secular world will more likely be on our side if we maintain such practices, which are, in the end, Christian practices.

Softening Hostility

Sometimes, of course, no matter what we do, no matter how diplomatic and loving we are, we're going to face stern opposition. That sort of thing happens to people who follow Christ. When it happens, though, I have found a few ways to soften the hostility.

• *Get face to face with opponents.* One neighborhood block club opposed our church because our development corporation was buying up empty lots and vacant buildings. After the building was gutted and remodeled, people from our church, some of whom were white, were buying them. The block club complained we were taking over the neighborhood, pushing black people out, moving white people in.

When the criticisms became pointed, I asked the club president if I could meet with him and then later speak at a block club meeting. I assured him, "There are no questions you can't ask me."

We didn't resolve all the tensions at those meetings. There are some people who still question our motives. But face-to-face encounters helped.

• *Do the little things.* One agency that helped fund some of our programs began questioning some of our methods. One afternoon we had a long, sometimes heated, discussion, but we didn't resolve our disagreements.

After the meeting, though, I sent each member of this funding agency a note saying, "I appreciate your work in this agency, and I'm impressed with the many good things this agency is accomplishing."

Small acts of kindness like this reduce friction, show goodwill, and "overcome evil with good" (Rom. 12:21).

Another time, neighbors across the street from our church became angry about some of our activities: we were too noisy; too many kids were wandering around the neighborhood. They even complained to the alderman about our "insensitivity."

A month after they made that call, however, they asked us if we would let them borrow a few folding chairs. It would have been easy to say, "Sorry, our chairs aren't available." Instead, we lent them the chairs and by doing so smoothed the relationship.

● *Pray not only* for *but* with *opponents.* Whenever I finish talking with our alderman, whether we are angry with each other or not, whether we're at City Hall or the local ward office, I ask, "Can we pray?" I have never been refused. If the circumstances seem appropriate, I've done the same thing with others. I've found that praying together with my opponents keeps our conflict less heated.

● *Focus on the opportunity.* The school prayer issue doesn't concern me. Kids can pray in school anytime they want. The only thing prohibited is adults forcing kids to pray. Instead of an obstacle, in fact, I see a tremendous opportunity: for young people to minister at their schools.

Before I started Lawndale Community Church, I taught at Farragut High School, located in the same neighborhood as our church. I also coached the wrestling team. The team prayed before each meet, but it did so at the initiative of the co-captains. One season, nearly every boy had committed his life to Christ. Again, it was the work of the co-captains, whom I had merely discipled. They led the team spiritually.

Often government regulation or neighborhood hostility is simply an opportunity to develop new ministries that involve new people.

Sitting in my office with the alderman and an angry block club president, with a mound of dirt in our parking lot, it seemed there was nothing I could do to turn aside the hostility.

Then our alderman, convinced that our church had exhausted every means to solve the problem, made an offer: "Can we get rid of this dirt for you?"

"Sure!" I said.

"Monday I'm going to have the Chicago streets and sanitation equipment here."

On Monday morning, two huge front loaders and eight semis showed up, accompanied that first morning by the alderman. Working daily, it took the workers two weeks to remove the dirt.

Like that mountain of dirt, some opposition seems as if it will never go away. But if we face it as Christ commands, loving both friends and opponents, our opponents — and even the alderman! — may eventually be won over to our side.

I don't need to trade away forthright, biblical messages for something faddish or trendy. People have a basic spiritual hunger that only faithful biblical preaching can satisfy.

— Ed Dobson

CHAPTER TWO

Speaking Truth in a Relativistic Society

The audience at our Saturday night outreach service is one-third unchurched individuals, one-third church dropouts, and one-third church adherents, so the majority come from a secular viewpoint. At the end of the service, I respond to their written questions; I have no idea beforehand what they will be. Questions range from predestination to masturbation, from abortion to suicide, and my answers aren't always what people want to hear.

One evening someone wrote, "I'm gay, and I've always been gay. Is that okay?"

"What you're really asking," I responded, "is 'What does the Bible say about human sexuality?' The Bible teaches that sexuality is a gift from God to be experienced within the commitment of heterosexual marriage. My understanding of the Bible is that all expressions of our sexuality outside of those boundaries are not within God's creative intent.

"Are you asking me if it's okay to have homosexual feelings? Yes, it is. But Scripture does not permit you to follow through with those feelings as a legitimate expression of sexuality. If you try to ignore that fact, there are consequences, one of which is displeasing God."

Answers like that can irritate people who don't accept an absolute standard of truth. One man said to me, "I really like Saturday night, but when you answer those questions, I wish you would quit referring to the Bible and tell me what *you* really think."

I congratulated the man on being so perceptive. The point of our seeker-sensitive service is not to tell people what I think but to help connect them with biblical truth. In a culture committed to relativism, hostile toward notions of unchanging, ultimate truth, the gospel can be an offense, no matter how positive my presentation. Sometimes that can't be avoided.

But sometimes it can. I've found that I can gain a hearing for the truth of the gospel, even in a relativistic culture. As I've conducted seeker-sensitive services and befriended non-Christians, I've gathered several principles for reaching skeptics with the truth.

Explain Why

The spirit of individualism, rather than community, dominates our culture, giving relativism a strong appeal. "You believe what you want, and I'll believe what I want" is the spirit of the times.

If a couple on *Donahue* says, "We've been married sixty years, and we're still happy," the audience applauds. But if they say, "We believe everyone should remain married for a lifetime," they'll get booed off the set.

Pervasive individualism has an upside. People want what

enhances their lifestyles, so I can reach them if I demonstrate that the values I teach are truths beneficial to anyone. I must show the modern skeptic the practical wisdom of biblical principles, particularly those principles that appear rigid or intolerant.

For example, to most people on the street, "Don't be unequally yoked" is the most ridiculous, narrow-minded idea they've ever heard. In their mind, if two people love each other, that's all that matters. They would think it silly, even tragic, for religion to interfere with love.

When I'm speaking on this subject, I focus on the logical reasons behind the scriptural principle: "You can't build a house on two sets of blueprints. In marriage if one person operates on principles rooted in Scripture, and the other operates on another set of values, it's only a matter of time until they collide over how to raise kids, spend money, or use leisure time. Sooner or later competing sets of values are going to hit head on. God understands that. He warns against being 'unequally yoked' because he wants couples to avoid painful conflict."

Secular people respond to good reasoning.

Appeal to Listeners' Curiosity about the Bible

While many secular people reject the notion of absolute values, they are curious to know what the Bible says. And if they have come to church, I assume they have at least some interest in biblical teachings or they wouldn't be there in the first place.

When answering the questions of seekers and skeptics, I nearly always preface my remarks with "If you're asking me what the Bible says, here is the answer." If I dodge and weave around the Bible, my audience won't respect me. Sometimes I must frankly say, "I may not like the Bible's answer, you may not like it, but this is what it says."

One Saturday evening a question read, "I'm a Christian. My brother was not a believer when he committed suicide. I still believe he'll be in heaven. What do you think?"

"What you're asking is whether the Bible gives several options on how to get to heaven," I responded. "I have to be honest with you. Scripture says Christ is the only way to heaven, and there are no other options. You are probably thinking, *So what does that mean for my brother?* Since you are a Christian, you undoubtedly had some influence on him; perhaps before he made this horrible choice he did turn and commit his life to Christ."

I would have loved to assure that man his brother was waiting for him in heaven, but I couldn't. I concluded, "If you're asking whether people can go to heaven without accepting Christ — no, they cannot. I'd like to tell you it doesn't matter, but if I did, I would be dishonest with the Bible." People respect that level of integrity.

Sometimes people are surprised by what the Scriptures say. People often ask me, "I'm gay; will I go to heaven?"

"Whether you're gay or not has nothing to do with whether you will go to heaven," I say. "It's a non-issue. The only relevant issue is the nature of your relationship with Jesus Christ. Have you placed your faith in him as your personal Savior? That's the sole criteria by which God will judge every human being."

I try to satisfy people's natural curiosity about the Bible in two ways. I preach verse by verse on Sunday mornings, and on Saturday night I use the Bible to answer topical questions. By going through a book a verse at a time, I'm eventually going to bump into the issue that concerns an individual. The questions on Saturday night force me to deal with listeners' urgent concerns.

Know Your Essentials

We gain a hearing with a secular audience when we don't confuse essentials with non-essentials.

One summer night we held our Saturday night service downtown, outdoors. We had just started when a ruckus broke out at the back of the crowd. It turned out to be a group of angry Christians staging a protest; they hoisted signs proclaiming that Christian rock music was of the devil. They became so disruptive the on-duty police patrolling the event arrested them.

Meanwhile eighty "punk rockers," attracted by the music, were sitting on a wall nearby, listening to my message.

No doubt the protesters were sincere in their beliefs about

rock music, but they failed to see their preferences about music were not on the same level of truth as biblical absolutes. (No one has yet shown me where Scripture explicitly condemns rock music.) I believe that is going to prevent them from having any effective outreach with unbelievers.

This not only affects how we go about evangelizing but what and how we preach and teach. When preaching or answering questions on Saturday night, I periodically make a distinction: what someone believes about Christ and the nature of salvation is far more important than what they believe, let's say, about women's ordination. I lose respect with outsiders if I were to treat both of those topics with the same level of authority.

Actually, I try to distinguish between three types of truth: absolutes are truths essential to the faith, truths that never change; convictions are nonessential truths over which orthodox Christians may differ; preferences are traditions or customs, like musical tastes, that may be compatible with the Bible but aren't biblically based, and they may change with the culture and over time.

Naturally, sometimes people will differ about which category a subject belongs to, but most issues seem to fall cleanly into one category or another.

Don't Skip the Tough Topics

I was flying back from California one day, sitting in an aisle seat across from some businessmen. One of them happened to notice I was reading my Greek New Testament and asked, "What language is that?"

"Greek," I replied.

"What kind of Greek?"

"New Testament Greek."

"That's amazing," he said. "I studied Greek when I attended a religious college in the Midwest. Why are you studying it?"

"I'm preparing for my sermon on Sunday."

"Really? What are you speaking on?"

I paused at that point. I looked at all his buddies sitting next to him, half-listening to our conversation. Did I really want to break the news to him in front of all his friends? But I knew I had to be honest with him.

"Well, Sunday morning my subject is hell," I said.

That was the end of the conversation for the rest of the flight.

When you're trying to gain a hearing from a secular audience, it's tempting to water down demanding Scriptures or avoid them altogether. We're afraid people will tune out of the rest of the sermon.

But I've discovered that's a mistake. Just when I think I know what the culture wants to hear and what it doesn't, I'm surprised all over again. Our most popular Saturday night series was entitled, "What Does It Mean to Be a Christian?" By any measure — attendance, audience response, or follow-up — it was the most successful four evenings in our Saturday history. Until then I had dealt with subjects like depression, bitterness, and forgiving your parents. The last thing I expected was an overwhelming response to such a simple, straightforward topic.

I learned a valuable lesson. I don't need to trade away forthright, biblical messages for something faddish or trendy. People have a basic spiritual hunger that only faithful biblical preaching can satisfy.

I've found that I can even preach about the most sticky of subjects, as long as I balance the troubling message with one of good news. We did a two-part series on Saturday night, one on heaven and the other on hell.

We introduced the subject of the afterlife by telling near-death experiences from popular literature. I wasn't prepared to say these experiences were real, but I pointed out they often paralleled the biblical teachings on death and the afterlife. The evening on heaven was well received.

But the next week, I said, "What I didn't tell you last week was there are other near-death experiences described in the literature that are not so pleasant. In fact, it's incredible how much these experiences parallel what the Scriptures say about hell."

I could tell people were uncomfortable in that second session, but they listened very intently.

Establish Authority

I suppose in earlier generations most preachers could assume their listeners conferred to them a certain level of authority. Many preachers could also assume their congregations had a minimal level of biblical knowledge.

Today I take nothing for granted. I assume virtually everyone will question virtually everything I say. Furthermore, I assume most listeners know little if anything about the Bible.

But how do you establish authority with a group that grew up on the maxim, "Question authority"? I've discovered such people will view me as credible if I do the following:

● *Let the people do some talking.* On Saturday evenings, we always take five to eight minutes to let someone share what God has done in his or her life. Listeners will accept my message if they see that it makes a difference in someone who doesn't get paid to spread religion.

I recently renewed the vows of a couple who had been on the brink of divorce. The husband had been living with another woman for over a year. The divorce decree was about to be granted when they both started attending Saturday night services independently of each other. They both ended up committing their lives to Christ.

The husband soon broke up with the woman with whom he had been living. The estranged couple began talking again. They eventually decided, "Hey, if God can forgive us, we can forgive each other. Let's start over again."

So in front of their unbelieving friends, they renewed their vows. I went to the reception afterwards. It was fascinating to hear their unsaved friends try to figure out what had happened to this couple. Out of that experience, several of them began attending our Saturday night service. They couldn't deny the difference Christ had made in the lives of these two people.

● *Practice what you preach.* The Scriptures say we can silence the foolishness of ignorant people by our good behavior. That involves going places Christ would go and spending time with people he would spend time with. I've said from our pulpit that if Christ were in my city today, he probably wouldn't attend my church. He would be down among the poor and dispossessed.

That's one reason we've gotten involved helping people dying of AIDS. When the AIDS resource center of Grand Rapids hosts their annual Christmas party downtown, some of us from our church attend. Such events are a great opportunity for ministry. At one of those parties, I met a woman dying of AIDS who had two children also diagnosed with the virus. I was able to talk with her about Christ's love.

Our church donates money to cover burial costs for those who die of the disease with no funds left to their name. In addition, each Christmas the AIDS resource center gives us a list of names of people suffering from the disease (first names only because they wish to remain anonymous) and a wish list that we distribute to our people. We gather the gifts, and when we give them the recipients know it's Calvary Church that donates the presents.

Our involvement with AIDS sufferers has built credibility. It's not uncommon for our Saturday night services to attract large numbers of seekers from the gay community. Women have stood and said, "I'm a former lesbian. Christ changed my life through this church."

● *Accept people as they are.* One Sunday morning a man walked into our morning service with the F-word printed on his tee shirt. That wasn't easy for many to swallow. As I heard later, when people stood to sing the first hymn, many couldn't get their minds off his shirt.

But as inappropriate as wearing that shirt was, it was important that we accept that man where he was. When the church requires that people clean up their lives, dress, and act a certain way before we will love them, we lose the respect of our culture.

So I remind our congregation that Jesus showed compassion to a maniac living naked among the tombs. Christ cared about him just as he was. So anything above nakedness ought to be acceptable dress code in our midst.

One evening I presented a man to the board who was wearing his hair in a long rat tail. He had contracted AIDS through years of intravenous drug use. He began attending our Saturday night service shortly after accepting the Lord.

"I don't know how much time I have left," he told the board, "but what time I do have I want to live for the Lord." By the time he finished, the entire board was weeping. They gathered around him, laid hands on him, and prayed for his future.

Any church that practices that type of Christianity will win the respect of outsiders and gain a platform to be heard.

● *Keep the playing field level.* Someone once complained that our church was soon going to be run over with homosexuals. I responded, "That would be terrific. They could take a seat next to the gossips, the envious, the greedy, and all the rest of us sinners."

I try to communicate that same attitude in my preaching: we all stand under God's judgment and we all are in desperate need of his grace. Letting people know that I'm not speaking down to them from some lofty moral position helps them listen to what I have to say.

● *Don't pretend to play God.* That means I have to be honest with people when I don't know the answer to their questions. A woman once asked, "Where was God when my father was molesting me?"

"I wish I knew where he was during your ordeal," I answered. "I just don't know. But I do know this: God loves you and wants to heal the wounds of your past." It's ironic, but not having all the answers helps people better trust the answers I do have.

● *Use the culture to introduce Good News.* Secular people know popular music, entertainment, and news media. So I've used such worlds to help make the Christian case. In my messages on Saturday nights, I cite secular studies, read from secular news sources, and quote from popular music to bridge the listener's world to the Scriptures.

On the night I addressed the theme, "Is there something in this world to believe in?" I showed the music video "Give Me

Something to Believe In," by the group Poison.

On another night, I used John Lennon's famous video, "Imagine." I asked the audience to imagine a world with no competing religions, no wars, no fights, where complete peace and harmony reigned. "Will there ever be such a place?" I asked. "Such a world is only possible through Jesus Christ, who gives us personal peace and changes hatred into love."

One evening we showed a film clip (with the unsavory language edited out) from a Burt Reynolds film entitled "The End." It's about a man with terminal cancer who is afraid to die. He keeps trying to commit suicide but chickens out at the last moment. His prayers of desperation resonate with the fears most people carry of death.

Explode Stereotypes

People in our culture hold many misperceptions about Christians. When I explode those negative stereotypes, primarily with humor, and perhaps satirize now and then the real foibles of Christians, I gain credibility.

One Easter morning, knowing many unchurched people would be in the audience, I wore my doctoral robes to the pulpit. Standing in this long, flowing black robe, I began my message, "In case you're watching by television this morning, I'm not Robert Schuller. This is Calvary Church." Once the laughter died down, I pointed to the various parts of this beautiful robe — the colors, the hood, the sleeves — and explained what each symbolized. Then I unzipped the robe and stepped out in a tee shirt and blue jeans. People gasped.

"On Easter Sunday, we all put on our robes," I said. "By that I mean we all get dressed up. We all put on our best image. But underneath all the hype, at the blue-jeans level, we often are very different people. We need to ask, 'Does Easter make a difference?' "

On another Sunday, I tied my hair, which I had let grow, in a pony tail. The idea that Christians ought to look and dress a certain way was another stereotype on my hit list. In a community as conservative as ours, that was pushing the envelope.

I finished my sermon, "I'm sure some of you are outraged that I wore my hair in a pony tail. But are you just as upset that your neighbors don't know the Lord? We get bent out of shape over things that have no eternal significance. But can we get equally agitated over people dying of starvation and millions who have never heard the gospel?

"I'm going to cut off my pony tail this week. My question to you is 'What are you going to do to show compassion to this world?' "

When I was a young pastor of a Baptist church in the mountains of Virginia, we started with only thirty-three people. *Seeker sensitive* wasn't even a term then. Instead we used gimmicks like "Water-Gun Sunday." But the leading moonshine bootlegger in that area came to know Christ. Soon his wife and children became believers. One Sunday I counted fifty people he had brought with him.

Reaching out to committed unbelievers is a great challenge requiring creativity and dedication. Sometimes the results are slow in coming; sometimes we have to endure a lot of misunderstanding and hostility. But sometimes the results are remarkable.

The pastor is the link between what's happening in therapy and God's Word.

— Louis McBurney

CHAPTER THREE
Ministry in a Recovering World

Years ago a pastor attending Marble Retreat was trying to climb out of deep despair. Several years before coming to Marble, she had taken her personal struggles to a psychotherapist and wound up in bed with him. Her troubles, as you might imagine, compounded exponentially.

In one of our first counseling sessions, I asked her what seemed like an obvious question.

"How have you dealt with your sin of adultery?"

A funny look crossed her face. "No one has ever called it that before," she said. "But it is sin, isn't it?"

"Yes, it is."

Right there she repented. It was the catalyst to her recovery.

Later, the irony hit me: this pastor's adultery had happened several years back, but apparently nobody in her church, denomination, or circle of friends had mentioned that what she did was a sin. Neither had the professional counsel she had received after her affair. I was flabbergasted.

A Little History

The North American church has been invaded by what some call the "therapeutic culture" — a culture that promotes openness, acceptance, and tolerance; a value system of listening, empathy, and support.

This phenomenon began in the 1960s, in what psychiatry called the Age of Anxiety. The cultural unrest of that period conceived and gave birth to despair, a despair that has continued for some thirty years. Today's lonely crowd has lost the capacity to cope. Many feel hopeless and aimless. The evening news reports the grim result: suicide, child abuse, spouse abuse, divorce, violence — the rates in recent years have skyrocketed.

Paralleling this despair has been the proliferation of support groups and professional counselors — the secular recovery movement — which provided many hurting people a safe, structured environment for dealing with their problems. By the late 1980s, in fact, seeing a counselor or attending a support group was considered chic: you had a doctor, a lawyer, *and* a therapist.

What began in the general culture, then, spread (some would say metastasized) to the church. Local churches allowed AA groups to meet in their facilities and sponsored support groups on divorce recovery, grief recovery, and overcoming sexual and drug addictions. Each spring Christian schools now graduate an army of counselors outfitted to help people work through their problems. These soldiers of healing find their way into local church settings or start counseling businesses. The language of recovery saturates the Christian air waves. At Christian bookstores, believers hungrily buy millions of dollars of self-help books that tell how to set boundaries, identify anger, and discover patterns of family sin.

In short, the landscape has changed.

These changes have affected how pastors feel about what they do. With parishioners getting help from counselors armed to the teeth with the latest psychological insights and filling up support groups, pastors can feel threatened. Their skills may seem obsolete. Leading Bible studies, preaching, visitation — these seem to be anachronisms. *What good am I*, they begin to think, *if people are getting all their good stuff from their support group? What's my role around here, anyway?*

One pastor who came to Marble said, "I'm supposed to be leading these people, but I've never experienced their various problems." He felt like an outsider: everyone was "recovering" except him.

What are we to think of this new phenomenon? How can we resist the culture's gravitational pull to overlook sin but at the same time maximize the ministry opportunities this new openness affords?

Balancing the Pendulum

While some pockets of the church have embraced the recovery movement, others have criticized it heavily, and for good reason. Many elements of popular psychology are clearly at war with Scripture.

No doubt it is laced with narcissism. Self is often exalted above all. The word *sin* is no longer used. Many efforts to help people with their problems completely ignore the spiritual dimension. Everyone is a victim. Parents, spouse, genetics — these all get blamed while individuals in therapy seem to be absolved of responsibility.

But I'm not prepared to wash my hands of psychology. The tendency is either to reject or embrace it. I'd like to suggest a third approach: reject the non-Christian elements and embrace the principles that help individuals exhibit the fruit of the Spirit. In fact, if applied wisely and in partnership with Scripture, I believe many psychological principles can lead people down discipleship's road.

Here's one helpful technique of therapy, for example, that

breaks entrenched patterns of sin. Let's say someone comes to me who is struggling with pornography. Using behavioral modification principles, I point out the pattern or steps leading him to sin: the stimulus, immediate response, and habitual behavior. A stimulus might be his feeling anxious or tense or depressed. His immediate response is to seek release from that discomfort. And through the years, he's developed an entrenched habit that acts like a tranquilizer: watching pornomovies or flipping through *Playboy* and then masturbating to release his anxiety. As soon as he feels a certain level of anxiety, the dominoes begin to fall: anxiety, pornography, masturbation. The pull is inexorable.

When asked, men who fight this problem can often tick off, with great precision, the events leading up to their action. By pointing out these patterns, I help a man identify the early stage, say, when he begins to feel anxious or tense. The stimulus will still be there — he still may feel anxiety — but his habitual response can change. Being aware of the dynamics and creating a new habit can halt the stimulus/response/behavior chain. As soon as he recognizes what is happening, he can pray, read Scripture, or talk to a friend. In short, he acquires one of the fruits of the Holy Spirit: self-control.

Not only does recovery have practical benefits, it also builds community. Our culture creates loneliness. In an age of despair, people need more than ever a place of hope, where it's okay to admit your problems, where people accept you, where "everybody knows your name."

That's the genius of support groups, a tool we have found beneficial at Marble Retreat. The pastors and spouses who sign up for two weeks of counseling and support at Marble have been emotionally beat up and bruised by adultery, marital struggles, pornography addiction, burnout, depression, and the vicious sheep in their flock.

For two-week periods, four couples meet together regularly with ample time for group sharing. We encourage participants to let down their guard and share frankly without fear of recrimination. The groups provide a safe place where any feeling is allowed and unconditional acceptance is the only rule.

One pastor came to Marble with a truckload of anxiety. Both his ministry and marriage were hung up on the rocks of self-doubt. He felt extremely ineffective and threatened as a person and as a minister. Over the days he spent with us, childhood problems bubbled to the surface, deep-soul issues of acceptance and identity. As he grew up, his parents gave him uniformly negative messages. When he found Christ as an adult, his life had turned around, but he still agonized over his worth and adequacy.

His time at Marble was a turning point. The group helped him to see himself in a different light, affirming who he was in Christ and telling him what they appreciated about him. One of the discussion questions the group was asked was simply, "What's new?" That simple question came to have profound significance for him. It became the symbol of change in his life. In a recent letter, he wrote:

"Well, what's new? Me! That's what's new. Those first three words have had a powerful impact upon my life, and those last four words are just beginning to sink in. I thank the Lord for the freedom I am beginning to experience. For example, I often found myself calling myself 'dumb' or 'stupid' when I would forget something or mess up. I still do that, but I find it's merely out of habit. When I do it now, there is no power in those words, and often I find myself chuckling about it.

"I'm really starting to like myself, and it sure is neat. I'm beginning to see that I have worth and not because of who I am or what I do, but simply because God loves me. Can you imagine that? God loves me! I must tell you that it's great to be loved. . . . And what is so neat is that God rescued me because he delights in me (Psalm 18:19). He delights in ME!"

His letter thanked all the group members for helping him understand God's love. This is just one element of the recovery movement within the church that offers a fresh and unparalleled witness of the gospel.

Therapy *and* the Word

However, the "new world order" in the church places new burdens on church leaders. Today's church culture, for example, puts a premium on pastors who are warm, relational, and vulnerable. What many churches want in a pastor is an empathetic support group leader: a healer who listens first, then makes poignant insights into people's lives, nurturing them on down the road to emotional health.

Not every pastor is wired for that. Nor should they be. Though the ground has shifted, pastors must stick to being pastors. Someone must still point to the Word and to Christ — that's always been included in the job description of a shepherd. What's happening in counseling and support groups must be linked with God's Word. Here are several ways to make that happen.

● *Encourage people to outgrow their status as victims.* Children naturally interpret their world as orbiting around themselves. In a home, say, where the father gets drunk repeatedly, causing chaos and turmoil, a 5-year-old child can easily come to believe, on an emotional level, that she is responsible for her daddy's problems. *I must be a bad person,* she thinks, *for allowing this to happen.* She grows up feeling responsible for not only her daddy's problems but also her husband's and those of other significant people in her life.

Years later, let's say, she finally gets into counseling. An initial step in therapy is helping the patient get in touch with her brokenness. She begins to see she wasn't responsible for her father's rampages. This revelation often causes a geyser of anger and resentment to spew forth — a necessary but painful step in the healing process.

While I may squirm at this anger, I shouldn't squelch it or encourage her to deal with it quickly. Anger itself is not sin. When these feelings are identified, talked about, and accepted as valid, only then should I encourage her to take the next step of releasing them in forgiveness.

Yet, take it she must. Too often people get stuck there. They stay angry and blame their parents and everyone else who has victimized them.

This is where pastors, in their preaching, counseling, and leadership, play an important role. They must lead their people to where they can say, "What happened to me was awful. I wasn't responsible for it, so I don't have to assume guilt or shame over it.

But neither do I have to be stuck there. The people in my life were fallen creatures just like me. They sinned and as children were probably sinned against.''

We should expect anger and resentment, but we must gently and slowly encourage moving towards forgiveness. This will require extra sensitivity on our part; we'll need to discern where people are in the healing process.

● *Link the recovered self with the serving Christ.* One of the most important but gritty tasks of Christian discipleship is moving people from being takers to being givers. In recent years, this has grown only more difficult. Those who have received counseling often feel released from the ought-to's and obligations that previously shackled them. As they get more in touch with their needs, which is necessary in the recovery process, they can become selfish, focused merely on their concerns.

To move beyond that, they must see themselves in relation to Christ. Their identity is not merely in discovering who they are but who they are in Christ. One is inward focused; the other, Christ-centered.

Simply put, who we are in Christ is this: redeemed sinners. When we absorb this truth, it leads to sacrificial giving. When we truly see who we are in Christ, we are freed from the pride of thinking we've done great things and also from the despair of feeling worthless. That change in focus reflects what Christ was modeling when he donned a towel and washed the disciples' feet.

I'm reminded of Frank, who handled his insecurity by arrogance and pretense. He perpetually brought the spotlight to himself and was jealously angry if anyone else was getting attention. After seeing the truth about himself, he was transformed. He stepped out of the limelight; he quit wearing flashy clothes and jewelry. He actually changed his first diaper, helped wash dishes with his daughter, went to his son's Little League game, and took out the trash.

He went on from there to helping in an inner-city soup kitchen where nobody knew who he was. He discovered the joy of self-giving service rather than self-serving performance.

● *Name sin.* Not long ago, a pastor and I were talking about Jesus' response to the woman caught in adultery: "Then neither do I condemn you. Go now and leave your life of sin." I had to confess to him that saying, "Neither do I condemn you," was much easier for me than, "Go and leave your life of sin."

While we're called to say both, the subtle pressure is to shy away from proclaiming the harder truths of the gospel. But pastors don't have that option. To link the healing process with genuine biblical discipleship, we must name sin. We cannot be complicit in one of the glaring errors of secular psychology.

In my counseling, I occasionally have to say, even though it cuts across my grain, "Cut it out. You've got power; you can control your behavior. You don't have to be a slave to these things." While empathy is important, sometimes the call for repentance is more urgent. At some point, we've got to say that their behavior is sin, that God is more powerful than that sin, and that repentance is required.

The Right Questions

One skill that helps us link a person's behavior to God's Word is asking the right questions. Our questions help people discover their deeper motives and explore what's going on inside.

I ask people questions like "What's the payoff for how you are acting?" or "What's in this for you?" I want to help people discover their underlying motivations. Then I try to help them see the real payoff of their behavior. When they do, they sometimes discover the payoff is decidedly negative.

Many pastors, for example, come to Marble completely frazzled and burned out — they are workaholics. Most workaholics never stop to consider the payoff of what they're doing. Questions like "What happens when you do this or don't do that?" force them to evaluate the consequences of putting so much time and energy into their work and so little elsewhere. Often they discover their drivenness originates in someone's comment that they're not good enough. They overlook three hundred compliments and become obsessed with one criticism.

So they push to prove otherwise. Often they're amazed to discover the bottom line of their workaholism. Our questioning can hold a mirror to their lifestyles and help them toward spiritual growth.

A common story for pastors who come to Marble is that of Tim. His great insecurities drove him unmercifully. He constantly had to prove his value, doing so by maintaining rigid control of programs and people. Though he pushed countless tasks to completion, he left many hurting people in his wake. He was unaware of what was happening and couldn't understand why his critics called him cold and insensitive.

We explored his attitudes about himself and how that affected his attitudes toward others. As Tim began to recognize that his sense of worth was completely wrapped up in his productivity and projects, he began to realize that he often felt irritated at people who got in his way.

Now, with a new foundation of self-worth in Christ, he can take time to hear others. He wrote that it feels so good to be able to listen to his parishioners, to understand them rather than feeling as though he had to give them a quick answer to get them out of his hair. He has a whole new vision for ministry, which now includes loving people and not just completing projects.

Caring

Before ending this chapter, I add three caveats necessary in a church culture of gaping wounds and infinite needs.

First, make sure you're helping people for their benefit, not yours. I entered medicine with a deep need to help others. Much of my makeup came from my mother's temperament. She is a natural caregiver who was trained as a nurse. To this day, she still loves to attend to the needs of her children. (And we all love having her mother us.)

Sometime during my medical internship, I realized a lot of my caring was for me, not for the person I was helping. I needed to be needed. That is a hazard for all caregivers, including pastors. We need to keep asking ourselves, *For whom am I doing this?*

Second, remember that the values of the recovery movement aren't always applied to the pastor. While people seem to want a friendly, transparent pastor, they also fantasize that their pastor is an all-powerful parent figure. They still expect their leader to be above their problems and sins, unencumbered by the same fears and doubts that swirl in their minds.

One pastor, before spending two weeks at Marble, had called off an affair and begun the hard work of repairing his marriage. By the time he and his wife arrived for help here, he was truly penitent.

Before he left, I advised him to come clean. I thought he should confess to his elders his sin and brief them on where he was in the healing process. I expected his leaders to show compassion, respect his forthrightness, and create for him a plan of restoration. He went home, confessed, and bared his soul.

The elders practically ran him out of town. He had to look for another job. Admittedly, adultery is a sin with heavy consequences that many believe disqualifies a man from pastoral ministry, at least for a time, but this pastor's revelation was not met with the virtues of the recovery movement. Pastors must take care what they share with the church.

Third, set limits on what you'll do for people. This is as much for their benefit as for yours. At Marble, the couples stay for two weeks in a lodge that is a hundred yards or so from my home. Often the couples will ask my wife and me to come over in the evening and visit.

Early in our ministry, we took them up on their offers. But we soon discovered on those evenings that the group deferred to me, the leader, and the group dynamics changed. The group stopped interacting and doing the hard work of processing the ideas they had been exposed to earlier in the day. When I stayed away, they had to depend on each other.

Likewise, if pastors become too involved in support groups and other recovery ministries, participants will look to them as the experts. The group loses in the end. They need to struggle to find answers; the hard work is necessary for healing.

We'll need to watch closely the number of hours we invest in certain individuals or the time spent with a couple in marital counseling. The best thing for them may be for us to back off, letting them learn to fly on their own.

The recovery movement has nudged many in our churches to take a hard look at their lives. Skeletons are being evicted from dark closets, and compulsions are being brought under control. Many are feeling a new sense of emotional and spiritual freedom. The problems that propel many people into counseling and support groups are, in effect, wonderful opportunities for discipleship. Our job is to steer them in the direction of the cross.

Unchurched people will have more respect for our public statements if we're not just talking about a problem but actually doing something about it.

— Ed Dobson

CHAPTER FOUR
Taking a Stand

$\mathbf{A}$ few years ago, I found myself having to rethink how I was to speak on controversial issues. A defining moment came after I appeared on Phil Donahue's television show in New York City. We were discussing a boy who had been denied membership in the Boy Scouts; he had refused to pledge allegiance to God, claiming he was an atheist.

I thrive on such confrontations. As a member of the Moral Majority, I had written the organization's platform. I had been invited to receptions at the White House, met privately with the

Vice President at his residence, and accompanied Jerry Falwell to meetings with foreign heads of state. The Donahue show provided yet another opportunity to engage in spirited, no-holds-barred discussion over moral issues.

The show went well. Afterward, with a strong sense of accomplishment, I hurried through the airport to catch my plane. Rushing down a concourse, I bumped into an older pastor whom I had known for many years.

"Where have you been?" he asked. With satisfaction, I told him about my television appearance. He didn't seem impressed. He rubbed his chin for a moment and then said, "Ed, you were called to preach the Bible, weren't you?"

"Of course," I replied.

"Then what are you doing here?" he said. "These talk shows are a waste of your time. They've diverted you from your primary calling. In my opinion, you're casting your pearls in the wrong place."

As I boarded the plane, I was unable to shake his comment. Nor could I shake it in the weeks and months that followed. For the next year my wife and I prayed over the direction of our lives.

The moment of truth came after the PTL scandal, when I was offered the presidency of PTL. That same day Calvary Church in Grand Rapids, Michigan, asked me to become their senior pastor.

That evening I went to my office and stayed the entire night to search my soul and seek God's leading. In the morning, it was clear what I should do. I accepted the call to Calvary Church in Grand Rapids.

I understood my primary call was not to address controversial moral and social issues in the media but to preach and teach the Scriptures and win people to Christ. I have never regretted that decision.

But I found I couldn't get away from controversial issues. We live in a controversial world that regularly touches the life of the church. In counseling, in church policies and practices, and in the pulpit, I am regularly called upon to address social and moral issues.

Now what? I knew how to do it on *Donahue*, but how was I to tackle these issues as pastor of a church?

Let the Bible Do the Talking

After the 1992 presidential election, I received a letter from a person alarmed at the political turn of events. "Pastor, the nation is in jeopardy," the letter said. "Yet you have been strangely silent on the issues threatening our society. Unless you stand up and lead this church in opposition to the new administration's policies, you will be partly to blame for the demise of our nation."

I called the individual and said, "I appreciate your zeal. If God leads you to take an active role in opposing political policies that threaten our moral foundation as a nation, that's terrific. But God hasn't led me to get involved on that level. I'm a pastor. I'm committed to evangelism."

I've learned that if I connect my ministry to a particular political party or adopt a protest mode, I immediately polarize people. I lose my opportunity to build bridges to groups who oppose my political positions. It becomes almost impossible for them to hear the gospel from me. I forfeit the ultimate mission of the church: preaching the Good News and making disciples of all nations.

I also told this man, "Furthermore, I'm committed to preaching the Bible. In our weekly pilgrimage through the Bible, when I come to Scriptures that speak to the issues that concern you, I will address them honestly and forcefully — and biblically."

That's the first principle, then, in tackling controversy as a pastor: let the Bible do the talking.

That means that I try systematically to preach through the Scriptures, rather than jumping from hot topic to hot topic in response to the evening news. This allows me to ground my teaching in the major themes of Scripture, so that when a controversial issue comes up in the text, people have a solid context from which to understand it. This also allows me to cover plenty of controversial topics, for the Bible is full of them!

This also means that when I do speak on a troubling issue, I do so exegetically, trying my best to found my views in biblical teaching. This grounds the issue in something larger than my own political agenda. And that not only gives me an objective basis on which to talk with others, it forces people to deal with the issue, and not just with me.

I once preached on abstinence and the use of alcohol in the Bible, and I ended up angering many in the congregation. I said that I personally practice abstinence. I offered seven compelling reasons why I believe every Christian should abstain from alcohol. Yet, to be honest with Scripture, I had to say there is great liberty for the Christian in this area. The Bible condemns only the abuse, not the use, of alcohol.

The next day a woman called. "Do you realize that every time a drunk driver kills a child in this area it will be your fault?" she said.

"Did you listen to the entire series?"

"Yes."

"Then tell me, at what point did I misinterpret the Bible?"

"That's not the issue," she retorted. "You are in a leadership position, and you have given people in our church permission to drink!"

"Wait a minute!" I insisted. "Tell me where I was wrong in teaching what the Bible teaches. If you can, I will get up next Sunday morning, admit my mistake, and apologize to the congregation."

Because her argument was with Scripture, I could compel her to think more deeply about the subject. Me she could just dismiss.

One temptation in preaching on contemporary controversy is to swagger — to get a little arrogant and assume your personal views are Scripture's views. Keeping the focus on the Bible has one other advantage: it keeps me humble.

I inherited my self-skepticism from my father. Just before I went off to college (to a school known for its dogmatism), he put his arm around me and said, "Ed, don't believe anything they tell you down there unless they can prove it from the Bible."

I've tried to teach my congregation the same principle. During a sermon I sometimes say, "Remember, folks, I'm fallible. Don't believe anything I tell you. You have a responsibility to judge from the Scriptures what I say. I can misread or misinterpret the Scriptures. So don't put your faith in me; put it in the Bible."

That attitude helps me not to speak for God when the Scriptures don't specifically speak to certain issues. For instance, I consider it the height of presumption to announce that AIDS is the judgment of God on the homosexual community. I am comfortable saying that if we sow to the flesh, we will reap corruption. That's far different from declaring that a specific virus is God's specific judgment on a specific group of people. Is AIDS also God's judgment on hemophiliacs, individuals who contract the virus through a blood transfusion or children born to a parent with AIDS?

The Gracious Prophet

Though I want to speak the truth, even about subjects that make us uncomfortable, I always want to be loving. That means a couple of things.

First, I don't blast people from the pulpit. For example, several members in our church are deeply concerned over the sex education curriculum in Grand Rapids schools. Some would undoubtedly like me to take aim on the public school system.

I opted for a positive approach. My wife visited the local schools and read the sex education curriculum for herself. She discovered to her surprise that the woman responsible for choosing the materials is a member of our church! If I had succumbed to the temptation to take a cheap shot at the school system, I would have wounded one of our own.

I would have also alienated the school superintendent, the assistant superintendent, and the hundred or so public school teachers who attend my church and attempt each week to be a witness for Christ in the public schools.

Heavy-handed preaching is also a mistake when it comes to the issue of abortion. Despite my firm opposition to the practice, I realize people are listening who have gone through that tragedy. Words cannot convey their painful emotions and memories. That's why I never address the topic without also explaining God's love, forgiveness, and grace.

Second, speaking to controversy in love means learning to find the middle ground where I can speak my convictions without trampling on others' convictions.

The church I now serve has historically been tolerant on the issue of baptism by immersion: in order to become a member of our church, you don't have to have been immersed. The problem, though, is that I believe immersion baptism is the proper prerequisite to joining the church!

How did the church and I settle that difference when I came on board? I agreed not to speak judgmentally about members who had not been immersed. In turn, the church granted me the authority to preach my convictions on this matter.

Finally, being a gracious prophet means sometimes being a little creative, even having fun while addressing serious issues.

One Saturday evening in our outreach service, we addressed a delicate issue: racism in the church. We introduced the topic with a skit about an older church member who volunteered to call on visitors. That night the man could not find his glasses, and his eyesight was so poor he did not realize that his first call was to a black family.

The visit went well, and he invited the family to his home for a meal. Just before he left, he discovered his glasses in his coat pocket. When he put them on, he was shocked to discover who he had just invited to dinner.

In a good-natured way, the black father chided him about the stereotypes some whites have of blacks. Underneath the humor was a serious message. Afterwards I spoke about racism in the church. At the end of the sermon, a black pastor from the community and I answered questions from the audience.

A local Catholic college had sent their minority-affairs staff adviser and members of the student minority council to the service. The next day they published a complimentary editorial in the school newspaper. In effect they said, "This is the first time we've seen a white church deal with the problem of racism in an honest way."

We could deal with it honestly because we had a little fun

along the way. That to me is a gracious and effective way to talk about tough themes.

Strategies for Church Change

Sometimes I've determined that I not only must speak about an issue but also that the church needs to act on it. That requires both grace and wisdom. Here are three things I keep in mind as I enter this risky process.

● *Start at the top.* Several years ago, I was struck by how Christ reached out and touched lepers, and I asked myself, *Who are the modern-day lepers in our society?* I concluded it was likely those suffering with AIDS.

Not long after that, I led to Christ a man with the disease. He was gay and had grown up in our church. Following his decision to receive Christ, I met with him for lunch on a regular basis. I tried to visit him in the hospital whenever he was admitted. A genuine friendship developed.

One evening I brought another person with AIDS to the church board to tell his story. It was a pivotal experience in our church life. That night AIDS became something other than a stigmatized and feared disease; it became a person to be loved and accepted. It's hard to maintain stereotypes and prejudice when you see how God can change a life.

My friend was a new creation in Christ, but he still had AIDS, and the board was forced to deal with the issue. We made two decisions: (1) to formulate a policy regarding AIDS in the church, and (2) to formulate a strategy to extend love to those suffering from AIDS. We would not wait for those with the HIV virus to come to us; we would go looking for them.

When a church moves into a controversial area such as AIDS, it must do so on solid footing. Church leaders must support it.

● *Follow a defensible process.* I try to follow an orderly process that can be defended once it's completed.

For a year and a half, our elder board reviewed our congregation's position on women in ministry. We spent considerable time studying the Scriptures, reviewing the literature on the topic, and discussing it on a board level. The board also met with a group of women who favored the ordination of women, a position different from the church's historical stance, and refined its stance based on their responses. At the end of that sixteen-month process, I stood before the congregation to preach on what became the most emotionally charged issue I had ever dealt with.

I made it clear these were not my views alone; they were the views of the entire leadership body. I acknowledged that at best, our position on women was a conviction, not a biblical absolute. Then I outlined for the congregation the process we had followed and finally shared the final conclusion of our study: we believed the New Testament supported multiple, male, godly church leaders.

Furthermore I said that, though portions of Scripture suggested women elders might have been present in the early church, the biblical evidence simply wasn't compelling enough to adopt that position.

I also said that churches that elect women elders or call women as pastors are not unbiblical. In fact, I admitted that we never could explain to our satisfaction the difference between women teaching an adult Bible class downstairs and standing in the pulpit upstairs.

"I'm glad the women mentioned in the Scriptures lived in biblical times," I said. "If they were alive in our churches today, they wouldn't have been allowed to do half the things they did."

Though we haven't come down in favor of the ordination of women, today three females are members of our professional ministry staff.

Still, some said we went too far, others said we didn't go far enough. Changes of that magnitude take time, so I let the congregation know that some policies would change immediately, while others would be phased in over a year or two.

Because we followed an orderly, thoroughly defensible process, we were able to alter our stand on an important issue and still maintain basic congregational unity.

Handling Public Conflict

Even though I no longer seek open confrontation with our culture over moral and social issues, there are times when conflict comes my way. When it does, I follow three rules.

● *Love thy protesters.* Peter said we can silence the foolishness of ignorant people by our good behavior. Sadly, we sometimes have the right position on an issue but lack the right spirit and demeanor.

Our church was sorely put to the test in this regard. One Sunday morning, protesters showed up outside our door, marching up and down our sidewalks denouncing the church and the Bible.

I walked outside and met with the protesters. I invited them inside for coffee and asked them to join us for our worship service.

"We'll come inside if you offer us equal time," they said.

"Our worship service does not operate by the Fairness Doctrine," I replied. "We can't offer equal time. But if you wish to come and listen, I'll be happy to meet with you after the service and answer any questions."

They refused.

Several of our people, though, had honked and yelled at the protesters on their way into the service. So at the beginning of the service, I gently corrected them. I said, "This morning I met with the picketers and asked them to join us in worship. They refused. Isn't it wonderful that in America we have the freedom to walk up and down in front of a church and protest?"

I saw a few individuals put their heads down. Afterwards several admitted to me that they had responded poorly to the unwanted visitors.

● *Media: Handle with care.* In my years with the Moral Majority, I discovered the enticement the media can have on a person. Seeing your name and words in the papers or seeing your face on television is seductive. Yet the results of high-level exposure are complicated, and the media can so easily ridicule your convictions so as to make you look like an idiot.

To help you avoid the wrong type of publicity, I offer the

following three suggestions.

First, resist the urge to provide the media with a sound bite. Reporters are always looking for a good story. They're out to find a fighting rooster who will get the feathers flying. Don't play that role; in the long run, it will hurt you and your cause.

Second, if you do choose to respond to the media, offer a well-worded, written statement. Period. Don't say anything beyond that, and grant an interview only if absolutely necessary. By all means, don't make generalizations. Preface your remarks by saying, "In my opinion," to avoid lawsuits. And stay away from attacking people on a personal level.

Third, remember that most of us pastors are not political experts. That's why we should stay out of most political issues. When a decision is made in Washington that sends reporters scurrying to your door for a comment, leave the door shut. In most cases, I don't return phone calls to newspapers.

On the other hand, if you do want to open the door to the media, show them firsthand the positive things you are doing to make a difference in people's lives: Thanksgiving dinners for people with AIDS, disaster-relief efforts, shelter for the homeless.

● *Keep your books open.* This is more of a prerequisite than a response to public criticism. If your finances are not open and clean when a public controversy arises, the media will surely begin to sniff around. Even if they find everything above board, the suspicion and questions they raise can make the church look bad.

To forestall all that, annually we publish financial statements and make them available to the public. We even print staff salaries. Full disclosure is one of the surest marks of integrity and accountability.

Actions Speak Louder Than Sermons

I've found that the most effective means of confronting controversial moral and social issues is to make these ministry opportunities. Unchurched people will have more respect for our public statements if we're not just talking about a problem but actually doing something about it.

Every time Mother Teresa visits the United States, she waxes eloquent on the evils of abortion, yet the press doesn't ridicule or dismiss her. Why? Because of her compassionate ministry to India's suffering. Compassion, far more than confrontation, impresses Christian and non-Christian alike.

So, when I'm asked about our stand on abortion, I explain not just our convictions but what we are doing about the problem. We are educating our junior and senior high young people how to deal with their sexuality. By encouraging abstinence and delayed gratification, we are helping them avoid having to make a decision whether or not to abort a child. In addition we support a women's center in the city; we help women carry their babies to term and to decide whether to keep them or put them up for adoption. We offer women a genuine alternative to abortion.

That not only impresses people, it opens doors for evangelism.

I once received a call from a local leader of Planned Parenthood who had heard about our involvement in finding housing for those dying of AIDS. "I don't know what's happening in your church," she said, "but everywhere I go I meet people who have been helped by your people. Whatever you're doing, keep doing it."

That phone call opened dialogue with someone in the "other camp." I oppose Planned Parenthood's stance on such issues as abortion and sexual ethics, but I had a brief opportunity to talk with one of their people one on one. And we talked not only about abortion and sexual ethics, but also about Jesus Christ — the ultimate controversial "issue," the one who makes the difference in all the issues we face.

Pressures on the Pastor's Family

Part Two
Pressures on the
Realistic Family

Often our expectations of spiritual intimacy are unrealistic or simply vague.

— Louis McBurney

CHAPTER FIVE
Why It's Hard to Pray with Your Spouse

A sick feeling takes over the pit of my stomach. The pastor's wife I'm counseling has just brought up a topic I'd rather avoid. Nancy is registering her hurt at the hands of her pastor-husband — and nailing me in the process.

"I remember how excited I was when we fell in love and I realized I was going to be married to a minister," she says. "I had always prayed for a godly husband, a man who would be a spiritual leader for me and our children. I was sure Joe would be God's answer to those prayers. We even prayed together on our dates. It gave me such a secure feeling.

"I just don't know what happened. After we married, all of that stopped. Oh, sometimes we still pray together or read the Bible, but only if I insist. That doesn't feel right. I want him to take the leadership for our spiritual life together."

I'm gulping hard and nodding knowingly — too knowingly. I've heard my wife echo similar concerns. This is one of my frequent failures: taking initiative for spiritual closeness in marriage.

Why is spiritual intimacy with my wife so easy to avoid?

Reasonable Excuses

I've discovered I'm not alone. Most of the ministers we counsel at Marble Retreat also struggle with this problem. It is another one of the pressures ministry leaders face, and it is intensified by both the secular culture (and its lack of interest in spiritual issues) and church culture, especially the special dynamics between a pastor and spouse. As I've worked with ministry couples, and my own marriage, I've seen a few common explanations (or excuses) emerge.

The first is the professional-exhaustion defense. It goes something like this: "I have to keep up this mask of religiosity almost all the time. From morning till night, I'm 'the minister.' I can't just be me. I'm always the one called on to pray everywhere I go. The only other guy that's prayed at Kiwanis in the past four years is Father O'Rourke. Men in the locker room health club apologize for cussing in front of me. I'm always expected to have scriptural answers for every question and deliver them with a loving smile.

"I get sick of it. Home is the only place I can relax and be real. I want to share spiritual things with my wife, but quite frankly, when she says, 'Can't we pray together?' I feel attacked. Then I feel guilty. Then I feel angry. Then I just want to escape."

I can't use this excuse, however; I'm a shrink, not a man of the cloth.

However, the second one, hypocrisy, does fit. My wife, Melissa, sees me offering sound spiritual counsel to others, but she knows I'm no saint. Sometimes I'm reluctant to pray with my wife because of this rationale:

"Melissa knows the real me. It's fine to offer holy solutions and wise biblical advice to others, but I can't get away with that at home. She knows I'm not very disciplined. She's seen my temper. She puts up with my pouts.

"She remembers the ways I've hurt her through the years by my selfishness or lust or thoughtless actions. She knows what I've been like as a father to our children. I'd feel like a total hypocrite expounding some Scripture verse to her or offering some pious prayer. She'd crucify me.

"No, it's safer to just play the game. She knows me too well. Maybe someday when I get my act together . . ."

Of course, the problem with that is I'll never get my act together. I need at least one place I can let down and be real. That seems more necessary than devotions.

The third factor is the spiritual-dwarf syndrome. Many male ministers believe, often accurately, that their wives are spiritual giants compared to them. A husband often feels dwarfed by his wife's deep faith. She doesn't seem to agonize with the same gut-wrenching doubts and questions as he does.

Her quietly committed prayer life shines compared to his hasty, often desperate prayers fired off on the run. The Word really seems to speak to her. Ages have passed since he has even read the Scriptures to find God's message for himself, and she wants him to be her "spiritual leader"?

How can he risk the vulnerability that spiritual union would bring? She would find out how shallow he really is. He feels less dwarfish behind the pulpit. Better stay there. It's definitely safer.

The other day a pastor friend told me, "I hate it when my wife asks me what the Lord has been saying to me. I've been feeling so spiritually dry, I'm not sure the Lord even remembers me. He seems to talk to her all the time, and that just makes it worse. I'm ashamed for her to know how far ahead of me she is spiritually."

Entering into real spiritual togetherness is a distinct threat to him.

Holy Disharmony

Another obstacle to spiritual intimacy is holy disharmony. Distinctive belief differences or style preferences may create dissonance when you try to pray, worship, or interpret Scripture together. Rather than unifying, it divides. You both agree with Paul that your joy would be complete if you were only of one mind, but that's about all you agree on. Common areas of disagreement include preference for time of day, interpretation of Scripture, devotional style, and issues of trust.

Melissa is a morning person, for example. For her, the most meaningful devotional experiences are flooded by the first rays of the rising sun. I'm pretty convinced, however, that God doesn't wake up till midafternoon. I'm sure the splendor of starlight was created to bathe our expressions of worship. That difference seems trivial until we try to adjust our biological clocks to find a time for devotional togetherness.

If your devotional time together includes reading Scripture, you may find tension in how you interpret what you read. One of you may thoroughly enjoy a lively debate, discussing various interpretations. The other may shrink from such encounters, preferring to find a practical application or an inspiring devotional thought. It is easy for a win-lose dynamic to emerge that quickly poisons the wellspring of shared spirituality.

For example, a couple at our retreat just had a doozy of a battle over what Ephesians 5 means regarding a husband's giving himself up for his wife. Her list of ways that applies was much longer than his.

Another difference is style. This includes the volume of words, the use of the language of Zion versus the vernacular, who does the praying, what resources are chosen, and what physical posture is preferred. Just as in corporate worship liturgy, our private devotional styles create a sense of comfort. If our mate's style is too divergent from our own, the feeling of genuine contact with God may be destroyed.

A friend of mine told me once that he couldn't pray with his wife. By the time they finished, he always rated his prayer at about a

6.0; his wife's prayer was of 9.5 Olympic quality.

The issue of trust encompasses concerns about what to ask God for and what to do yourself. Whether or not God wants to heal our physical illness may raise anxiety. How to seek God's will is often understood differently. Should we take risks trusting God to provide for our plans or should we not extend ourselves beyond the provisions God has already provided?

Most of the aspects of trust carry intense emotion since this is such a foundational element of our personality. Taking a cautious approach seems to be showing a lack of faith for more adventure-some souls, while to more "practical" believers leaps of faith seem irreverently presumptuous.

Is It Wise to Confess?

Another obstacle is the fear of confession. "Confess your sins to one another so you may be healed" sounds pretty good delivered from the safety of a pulpit. Applying it with your mate is a different matter. Just how confessional can you be without creating hurt or anger or doubt?

I want to be totally open with Melissa, but at times I'm reluctant to disclose all of the sins of my thought life. Can she hear about my lust without feeling rejected? She faces the same dilemma. Can I face her admissions without defensiveness?

Quite honestly, I'd rather confess to God or to my buddy, Doug, than to my wife.

Let me mention a final, common explanation of why pastors avoid spiritual intimacy with their spouses: spiritual stone throwing. At times, the only time marriage partners feel safe to confront each other is in prayer or through Scripture.

One pastor's wife told me recently, "I hate to have prayer with John. He begins right away to beseech the Almighty to reveal to me my sins: 'Lord, help Susan with her laziness. Reveal to her how she can be more organized. Create in her a spirit of submissiveness so she can be the godly woman you want her to be. Protect her, Lord, from the evil influences of television and the covetousness that stalks her in the mall.'

"I come away from our prayer time feeling flagellated and condemned. I think I'd rather be slapped in the face than deal with the guilt he heaps on me disguised as prayer. One of these days I'm going to pray that the Lord will reveal to him his judgmental attitude and lack of love. In the meantime, I don't want family devotions. Thanks, but no thanks!"

Steps Toward Spiritual Togetherness

So what's to be done? Most couples agree they need the sense of spiritual oneness. Wives particularly crave the feeling of closeness nurtured in prayer. Avoidance or a frustrated acceptance of failure doesn't bring much peace.

You don't have to remain stuck, though, in the ditch of spiritual estrangement. Here are some steps Melissa and I have found helpful for ourselves and others.

1. Identify the problem. Clear an afternoon or evening in your schedule to discuss this area of your relationship. Allow no interruptions, and covenant together to make understanding (not agreement) your goal. Enter the time without your usual agenda of proving who's right and who's wrong. Believe me, you both are — right *and* wrong.

Since who is in control is such a common marital conflict, it's particularly important to take conscious steps to avoid that dynamic. Lay ground rules giving each person time to speak and the responsibility of listening.

I frequently observe marital breakthroughs when couples suddenly release their old perceptions and assumptions. I hear, "Oh, so that's how you've been feeling," or "I didn't realize you wanted *that*." When defensiveness is abandoned, it's possible to hear and really understand each other.

Trace the history of your spiritual relationship, recalling the times it went well and the times it didn't work for you. Then try to identify how you've felt about having a spiritual conversation.

Your goal is to understand each other in a nonjudgmental way. You may be uncomfortable with what your mate feels, but accept her perception as the truth from which she acts.

2. *Clarify expectations.* I used to believe Melissa wanted me to be something I'm not. She would talk about her desire for me to be more of a spiritual leader for her. That sounded pretty overwhelming to me. So rather than risk embarrassment or failure, I'd avoid even trying. I interpreted her expectations as wanting me to lead in deep discussion of the Scriptures or to expound on some dramatic vision the Lord had given me (a fresh one for each day, of course).

When I finally told her what I thought she craved, she was flabbergasted. I'll never forget the relief I felt when she said, "Oh, that's not what I want. I just want a spiritual companion, not a leader."

Compare your childhood experiences with family devotions. Most of our expectations germinate in the rich soil of the family garden. The seeds of a disciplined but oppressive system may bear blossoms in marriage that look like weeds to a mate whose family had a freer style. Families who had no devotional patterns at all can create either a hunger for times together with God or a fearful resistance. When your childhood memories clash, then the bouquets of togetherness can lose their fragrance.

Often our expectations are totally unrealistic or simply indescribably vague. We may have developed an image of what spiritual sharing is supposed to look like from some conference or a book we read, but never stopped to define it clearly with our mate.

Nothing leads more quickly to frustration and disappointment than unmet expectations. When those ideals are present as a hidden agenda and not spelled out clearly, you can predict failure.

3. *Renegotiate a contract.* When I had a clearer idea of Melissa's expectations, I felt more comfortable working toward an agreement. What would look like "spiritual companionship" to her?

As it turned out, what she had been wanting was much easier than what I had been assuming. We began to spend a short time at breakfast reading Scripture (usually a paragraph or maybe a chapter), then praying together briefly about our individual concerns. It also helps when I talk about how the Lord is working in my heart. At times we get together for a longer period of prayer or discussion, usually when life's pressures seem to be closing in.

For Melissa the keys were two: that I would show enough interest to initiate spiritual conversation and that I let her peek inside my mind and heart. The first is accomplished by my reaching for the Bible when we finish breakfast. That's not too hard. The second is satisfied by my letting her know my prayer concerns. Looking back, it's sad we made such a difficult problem out of such a simple task.

4. *Avoid criticism.* You can be pretty sure that you're going to blow it somewhere along the way. You'll get busy or be angry with each other, or somebody will have the flu, and then you won't do it the way you intended. When that happens, refuse to place blame and judgment *anywhere*. That's deadly.

A couple at our retreat is struggling with bringing some positive change into their lives. Just yesterday, Joe said, "I've discovered that I'm resistant toward trying to change. I find myself feeling a lot of anxiety. I'm afraid that I won't be able to do it right, and then Sue will point out my failure. When that happens, I think, *What's the use*? and I look for somewhere to run."

Whatever you do, don't get into a courtroom debate over whose fault it is or over who wants to quit.

You can express your sadness that your time has been interrupted. "I really miss our spiritual time together" is enough. You might ask, "How can we get things going again?" If some of the old resistance has redeveloped, start over identifying the causes. Focus on yourself and what you may have contributed. Then apply grace to each other where it's needed.

5. *Celebrate your steps toward spiritual oneness.* Every time Melissa tells me how good she feels when I initiate sharing, I get a renewed commitment to the process. Our unity is reinforced each time we tell others about the importance of having a soulmate as our spouse — for example, when we're with friends and I tell them that Melissa and I were praying together for them the other day, or when she says, "Louis and I were just reading that Scripture recently."

Those comments are ways we let each other know how satisfying our spiritual closeness is.

Ours has been a rocky pilgrimage in this area. But we're finding a new sense of freedom and safety. Our growing spiritual oneness is helping us enjoy more fully the other dimensions of our lives together, whether long walks hand in hand or our sexual intimacy. It's still not easy, but the strength and joy we experience together makes the struggle worthwhile.

We don't do our children a favor when we protect them from the world.

— Wayne Gordon

CHAPTER SIX

How Much Should We Shelter Our Kids?

Thirteen years ago my wife, Anne, gave birth to our daughter, Angela. Two days later I proudly drove my Chevy to the front door of the hospital and assisted Anne and Angela into the car. Pulling away from the curb, we headed for the Chicago inner-city apartment where we had lived for three years.

When we crossed California Avenue and entered the Lawndale neighborhood with its glass-strewn empty lots and burned-out tenements, my wife began weeping.

"What are you crying about?" I asked. "This is a happy

moment." (The proud father got a failing mark for sensitivity that day.)

"How can we bring our innocent little daughter into this environment?" she sobbed.

I figured my wife's emotions had something to do with postpartum depression, but I also suspected her maternal instincts were on target. Though I am not often burdened by guilt, at that moment, I began to feel guilty about where I had brought my family for the sake of ministry.

Pressures on the Pastor's Family

Inner-city ministry isn't the only ministry that is risky to a family. Frequent moves can traumatize a spouse and children. Churches that openly criticize a pastor can leave a family bitter toward ministry. And then there are the many normal complications of church life. Let me note three.

● *Failed role models.* Several years ago, a popular young man, who eventually became a deacon in our church, was like a pied piper to the children. He spent considerable time with all the children, including mine, regularly taking them to the lake and the park.

Then we learned his girlfriend was pregnant. My children, who were in elementary school at the time, old enough to understand what was going on, began asking questions: "Dad, I thought you weren't supposed to have a baby before you were married."

"Dad, Bob (not his real name) is a Christian. He has always taught us about God, but now he is not obeying God. Don't we have to obey all that God teaches us?"

I saw my children confused and hurt.

That hasn't been the only time one of our church leaders has failed sexually, and each has shaken our children. Such failures, sad to say, are not uncommon no matter the church setting. The sexual temptation and unbiblical ideas about sex that our children absorb from popular media are bad enough; when children also get mixed messages in church, the pressure is that much greater.

● *Financial constraints.* We have a rule in our house about tennis shoes: Mom and Dad will pay forty dollars for shoes, and if the kids want to buy something more expensive, they can add their own money. Still, the most we'll spend on tennis shoes is a total of sixty dollars.

One day my daughter came home in tears wearing her fairly new, clean, tennis shoes. All her friends, who wear L.A. Gear, made fun of her because she was wearing a no-name brand.

A status symbol for my son Andrew is Air Jordans, with a price tag of $100. (And they can't just be Air Jordans; they have to be *this year's* model of Air Jordans.)

One day Andrew and I went to the mall to shop for shoes. He saw the pair he wanted, and I saw the price tag. "No way," I said. "You know the rules. We're not spending $100 on shoes. But we can shop around and see if any stores sell Air Jordans at a lower price."

We walked through the entire mall without success. "You're going to have to get a different kind of shoe," I finally said. He resisted. I tried to stay calm, but then I got angry. I pointed to a pair of less-expensive shoes and said, "Are you going to get these shoes or not?"

"No!" he snapped, and we charged out of the mall. We drove home in silence.

Later that night, I went into his bedroom to pray with him, as is our custom. "Andrew, what is the thing with these gym shoes?" I asked. "Do gym shoes make you a better person?"

"No," he answered. "But when you have those shoes on, everybody looks at you, and they know you're in style. It makes you feel good."

He started to cry. "If I don't wear those shoes, everyone will make fun of me!"

"Maybe they will," I replied. "But the important thing is what is inside you: your love for people and your love for God. If you grow up, and you're always looking to have the best suit, the best car, the best house, you'll be miserable."

Hoping my little sermon had won him over, I asked, "What

do you think?''

"I still want the Air Jordans."

"Well, you can't have them," I concluded. "If you want to get the other shoes, let me know." And I walked out of the room.

Early the next morning, I went to church for my devotions. The phone rang, and it was Andrew. "Dad, I thought some more about it last night. You're right. I want to get the $60 pair of gym shoes."

That was a long battle that ended on a positive note. But they don't all end so well. Frankly, it's hard for me not to spoil my kids.

● *Time pressures.* I have trouble getting home on time. I promise my wife and children I'll be home at, say, 5:00. But as the work piles up, I wait until 4:57 to dash out of my office door. Although it's only a two-minute walk to my home, because of the number of people I meet in the church and neighborhood on the way home, I'm fifteen or more minutes late.

Perhaps you've seen the T-shirt that says, IF MOM IS NOT HAPPY, NOBODY IS HAPPY. That's how it is at our dinner table when I'm late. Always being available for others but not available for our families takes its toll.

Several years ago while we were on vacation, my wife and I asked our two oldest children, "If you could change one thing about us, what would it be?"

"Well, Mom, sometimes you get a little irritable. It would be nice if you wouldn't yell at us when you get mad."

I breathed a sigh of relief. *It sounds like we're doing okay; every parent flies off the handle now and then.*

Then it was my turn. My son said, "Dad, I want you to be home more at night. You're never around. I never get to see you."

That hurt, but it wasn't a surprise. "Andrew, that's certainly a good point."

Then it was Angela's turn. "Dad, I wish you were someone I could trust. I don't trust you."

I was stunned. "What do you mean?" I asked.

"You tell me you'll do something, but you don't do it. You break your promises."

She was right. I had the best of intentions toward my children — "I'll read you a book tonight, Angela" or "We'll go to the lake tomorrow" or "I'll be home in time to help you with your homework" — but then I let church demands and people in need take priority.

Wherever we minister, our children will face such pressures. So how can pastors balance the parental instinct to shelter their families, and the call of God, which often leads them to challenging, even dangerous places? How much should we put our children in harm's way for the sake of a particular ministry? What do we sacrifice when we minister in difficult settings?

Too Much Shelter

The natural reaction when facing such risks is to build high walls of protection. But I don't believe we do our children a favor when we shelter them from the world. In particular, three important and necessary things happen when our children have to deal with these challenges.

First, they learn about life.

I was in the back room of our third-floor apartment, preparing it for a tenant, meantime keeping an eye on 6-year-old Andrew, who was playing with neighborhood boys in the back lot. I heard shouting, and I looked out the window to investigate.

One of the boys was on top of Andrew (and I later learned he had punched Andrew in the nose). At that moment, the other boys pulled the aggressor off Andrew, and I heard them say, "Don't you ever hit Andrew. That's Coach Gordon's son" (even though I'm a pastor, I'm known as "Coach"). I ended up having to go outside and stop them from hurting the boy who hit Andrew.

I don't like seeing my son with a bloody nose, but that experience was good for Andrew. The worst thing I could do in that circumstance is say he can't play with those boys any more. Life is full of bloody noses, and I won't usually be nearby to pull off the bullies.

Second, by facing the world, our children learn about ministry.

Whenever it's appropriate, I take my kids with me when I minister at places like Cook County Hospital, Cook County Jail, other churches, or with individuals in the neighborhood. My daughter walked the streets with me when I ministered in Harlem. Even though those places can be disturbing, they are places where children can develop the values of the kingdom, like the value of sacrificing for others.

One Saturday night in February, I came home at 10:30 after a church meeting. The kids were still awake. The phone rang, and the man on the end of the line said his car had broken down near the church. He needed $20 to fix it.

We discussed his situation a while, and I sensed he was giving me a line, so I finally said, "I don't have $20. We'll give you a ride home tonight, and on Monday we'll help you repair your car."

He wouldn't take no for an answer. I repeated myself several times and eventually was able to hang up the phone. I turned around, and there was my son Andrew, standing in his pajamas with a $20 bill in his hand.

"Dad, I want to give that man $20 to fix his car."

Andrew had celebrated his eighth birthday a few weeks before, and his grandparents had sent him money. For over a month he had held on to $68, unsure of how to spend it.

I had mixed feelings about Andrew using his money this way, but I said, "If the man comes back on Monday, I'll use your $20 to help him fix his car."

The man never did call back, and when I told Andrew, he was a little sad. He really wanted to help that man.

Third, seeing the world helps children become better Christians.

Bobby, one of our neighborhood drunks, regularly hangs around our church begging for money or lying on the curb intoxicated. One night I walked out of church with the kids, and Bobby leaned over, fell on me, and mumbled something. "We're going home, Bobby," I said.

After we had walked a few feet, Angela asked me, "What is the matter with Bobby? He can't walk, and he smells funny." (She had seen him before, but now she was old enough to ask the question.)

I explained that Bobby was drunk, that drinking had ruined his life, kept him from working, destroyed his family, given him the scars she saw on his face. Because of conversations like that, I don't worry about my kids drinking as adults. Seeing the real world and the consequences of disobeying God teaches them better than any Sunday school lesson.

While no method of raising children is foolproof — they always have a free will — and though exposing our children to this world has risks, my wife and I agree our children are better for it. We have had an invaluable opportunity to communicate our values and beliefs and to set an example of serving others.

When to Protect

Oversheltering is one thing; neglect is quite another. In spite of my general philosophy of allowing kids to be exposed to some risks, I still feel I need to protect them from some influences.

• *Serious physical harm.* My 4-year-old son, Austin, was playing in the back lot with his sister. Three teenage boys walked by, grabbed Austin, and pushed him hard to the ground. Angela carried Austin into the house, and when she told us what happened, I was furious. I ran out the back door looking for the teens. At a nearby park I asked people if they had seen them. Before long the whole neighborhood was on the hunt.

We never found them.

There is a huge difference between a boy getting a bloody nose from his peers and a 4-year-old being attacked by teenagers. My children don't need the latter, and Anne and I go overboard to prevent it. We always know our children's whereabouts and never allow them to roam the neighborhood. (Thirty-five people are shot every day in the city of Chicago.) If one of the kids wants to play with a friend two blocks away, Anne or I walk them there, or we watch them walk and ask the friend's parents to watch for them, meet them, and call when our child arrives.

My daughter is in eighth grade this year. We have already decided she will not attend the local public high school. Due to the risks of gang violence and rape, as well as the inferiority of the education she would receive there, we have ruled that school out.

• *Abuse.* When our children turned five, we counseled them about sexual abuse, teaching them the difference between good touch and bad touch. ("Bad touch is when anyone touches you where your underwear is.") We tell the children immediately to tell us if anyone is touching them wrongly. At our church we screen children's workers to guard against sexual abuse.

We also guard against emotional abuse. Although I want to raise my kids so they can handle what the world dishes out, I am sensitive to how certain situations are affecting our children's feelings.

For years our children rode the bus to school. One day we learned from Angela that on the bus Andrew was swearing and getting into fights. He was the only white boy on the bus, with the rest being Hispanic and African-American. The Hispanic kids began to taunt Andrew, who sat with the black kids, saying he was a "wanna be" (that he wanted to be black). This happened several times and led to the fights.

Finally at the dinner table, I asked, "What do you all think about riding the bus? Andrew, is it a safe place?"

Andrew did not ask to be taken off the bus, but he said it was not a good place for him. My wife and I thought and prayed, and we decided Andrew wasn't handling the situation well and needed more protection than we might normally give. We continued to have him ride the bus in the morning, when it didn't seem to be as much of a problem, but we started driving him and Angela home after school.

• *Television.* At our house, the rule is no TV on school nights. It's easy to let the TV serve as a babysitter or a way to get peace in the home, but it hurts the kids' school work. And frankly, I think too much television destroys morals. We have noticed that after our children watch a show with some violence in it, they tend to argue more.

When we first put the restrictions on, the kids complained a lot, but eventually they found other things to do, and the television lost much of its allure.

Tom and Nancy Johnson, friends of ours, help lead an inner-city ministry on the west coast. Once when Tom was out of town, Nancy was suddenly awakened in the middle of the night by a man on top of her. She began fighting for her life — screaming, scratching, punching.

The intruder cursed and tried to subdue her. The actual attack probably lasted less than five minutes — the intruder finally giving up and running out the back door.

That experience shook Tom and Nancy, and they seriously considered resigning that ministry. But they decided to stay, still feeling God's call to that ministry. "That night the level of protection wasn't what we wanted," they say, "but we know we're supposed to be here, and we still trust God for protection."

We live in a world of physical and spiritual dangers. No matter where we are, ministry has risks. I'm doing everything I can to prevent anything untoward from happening to my family. At the same time, I feel God's call to minister in a dangerous place. That call is winning out, and God has enriched my family as we have followed him.

If your wife resents you or the church, it isn't just her problem. You certainly share in the consequences.
— Louis McBurney

CHAPTER SEVEN
When Your Spouse Resents the Church

Travis's first couple of years at First Church as an associate pastor went well: he got along with the senior pastor with only a few, minor disturbances. By his third year, however, things began to deteriorate, and that began to affect his wife.

Travis was a maverick who shared most of the cultural symbols of his baby-boom generation. He had worn his hair long since adolescence. He dressed casually. He was "into" movies. He enjoyed contemporary music. His lifestyle seemed to run counter to most of the older, mainstream leaders of the congregation. Yet he was a loving, committed, effective minister having a noticeable impact on the growth of the church.

At first he displayed a defensive, almost rebellious attitude about the criticism coming his way. The people could accept him the way he was or ask him to leave! Finally he consented to wear his hair shorter, but he refused to wear a coat and tie in the office.

Not only was he a maverick in his lifestyle, he began to challenge the social stance of the church. He began an inner-city ministry that was attracting to the church people from lower economic levels. Church people felt showing concern for the homeless was one thing; sitting by them in worship was something else.

Worse than that, in some people's minds, was his lack of respect for denominational ties. The church had been the most prominent congregation in the state, the flagship of the fleet. Now this renegade staff member seemed to devalue that position. For that, he began taking heat from the church elders and other church staff.

Naturally, Travis confided in his wife. And naturally, Barb rallied behind her husband. Every time Travis came home discouraged or with a new twist in the unfolding drama, she saw red. A slow but steady frustration began to mount. She obsessed on how her husband was being vilified: *They're persecuting him and stabbing him in the back — after all we've done for this church!*

With no one besides Travis to talk to — even he became defensive when she criticized the church — she felt isolated and trapped. Over a two-year period, she quietly withdrew from her church commitments, including choir. She even stopped attending Sunday evening services.

Resentment in a pastor's wife is like a natural gas leak — often hard to detect and discovered only after an explosion. Most likely, when an explosion occurs, it's the result of a slow leak. Little things accumulate: financial stress, petty criticism, feeling unappreciated. Finally, often near midlife, some conflict or crisis ignites the pocket of fumes.

If your wife resents you or your work, at best it will cripple her relationship to the church. At worst, it can destroy your marriage or force you to leave your present charge. (Since most of the ministry couples I've counseled are male pastors and their wives, I'm assuming a traditional couple for this chapter.)

How can you spot resentment in your wife? What can be done to help her resolve her anger and prevent it from destroying your marriage and ministry?

Detecting the Leak

Before entering ministry, Bob was a civil engineer. In his early thirties, he felt a call to full-time Christian service. His wife, Mary, who shared his call, supported him enthusiastically. So they headed off for school.

Their first parish out of seminary was a small, rural church, and Mary fit right in. Both she and Bob loved ministering in a farm community. After three years there, however, Bob began to toy with the idea of moving onward and upward. When a larger, suburban church contacted him, Bob was ecstatic.

Mary resisted moving from the start. When Bob brought the subject up, she was forthright: she wanted to stay put. Their ministry was flourishing, she said. Why leave now? Bob promised her he would not accept the call without her green light.

One day Mary overheard Bob on the telephone telling a friend he had accepted the position at the suburban church. Feeling shocked and betrayed, she confronted him as soon as he got off the phone. "You promised you wouldn't accept that position unless I agreed!" she said.

Bob shrugged his shoulders. "I'm sorry, but I can't go back on my word," he said. "I'm sure you'll like the new church."

At first Mary felt hurt, then she got angry. But the show had to go on. Smoldering inwardly, she picked up and moved to her new station in life.

The church, as it turned out, was a nightmare for both but especially for Mary. Angry at Bob, she withdrew emotionally from him. Once warm and outgoing, she now was distant from Bob and everyone in the church. She busied herself with their children.

Within two years Bob resigned the church.

Mary's response is typical of an angry pastor's wife: with nowhere to go with her anger, she pulled into herself. Pastors' wives don't get even; they withdraw. With no one to confide in, they feel trapped and alone. And the insular world of church culture only magnifies the problem. She is the pastor's wife — and a pastor's wife isn't supposed to have problems. So she retreats into the woodwork.

Sexual disinterest is another form of withdrawal. In general, sexual intimacy for women is more relational and emotional than physical. At Marble, ministers' wives frequently tell us that when they feel angry towards the church or their husband, sexual intimacy is unimaginable: "How could my husband possibly desire intimacy when there's so much emotional distance between us?"

Resentment also commonly comes out in physical symptoms. An angry spouse is likely to start complaining of headaches, backaches, stomach aches, fatigue.

In some cases, however, resentment doesn't go underground. It manifests as unapologetic rage. One pastor's wife said, "I'm the world's worst bitch, and I know it. When my husband comes home, I start in on him because I'm so furious with him and his d——n church."

Another woman took out her anger by criticizing her husband in public. In small group meetings or when entertaining church guests, she made snide comments aimed at him. Still another stopped attending her husband's church altogether — a not-too-covert way of saying, "I'm angry, and you are going to know about it." Other wives express anger by overspending on credit. They are communicating, "I don't feel I'm being treated nicely, so I'll compensate by treating myself to nice things."

Flight or Fight

When the spouse is angry at her husband or his work, it feeds his insecurities. The pastor may think, *What if her resentment jeopardizes my ministry? Or puts a wedge between me and So-and-so in the church? What if I'm forced to leave this church — or ministry?*

He's tempted in one of two directions: to ignore it or become defensive. A pastor already feels he's peddling as fast as he can. When his wife complains about the pressure she's feeling, she becomes another problem. Going home gets to be a drag, so some pastors avoid the problem. They invest even more time and energy in ministry. The wife's cries for help fall on unsympathetic ears.

John and Becky threw themselves into their first church with idealistic abandon. After a few years, however, Becky grew disenchanted when one of the leading families of the church repeatedly criticized and hounded John. Unable to do anything without their blessing, John felt as if his hands were tied. Becky shared his frustration.

Then a woman from this dominating family began working as John's secretary. Soon she became more than a secretary; she acted as if she were John's associate pastor. For whatever reason, John allowed it to continue. She tagged along to his meetings, stayed at church to help when he worked late, and seemingly had a voice in every area of church life.

At first Becky tried to be the loving, supportive pastor's wife. Occasionally she mentioned that she was uncomfortable with the situation, but John would brush her aside: "Suzi is a wonderful addition to the ministry. I couldn't do it without her." Becky would drop the matter, but that didn't resolve her feelings.

Then she attempted to compete with John's secretary; she started spending more time assisting at the church office. She worked late with her husband. That's when Suzi, the secretary, said, with deep "concern" one day, "John needs more support at home than at church."

At the same time, Becky had sensed John's discomfort with her involvement; so she backed off. Then she completely withdrew. Over the course of two years, she quietly gave up on the church and, though remaining married, gave up on ever having a close relationship with John.

These were painful years for John, too, and he could have saved himself a lot of that pain had he not ignored or dismissed Becky's red flags. He never had a sexual affair with his secretary, but by the time he wised up, his marriage was teetering towards failure. In essence, he abandoned her. In doing so, he multiplied her insecurities and turned up the volume on her anger.

Defensiveness is just as bad as ignoring a problem. When his wife is openly critical of people in the church, a pastor may say something like, "They are just sheep who need a shepherd. You'll have to put up with their comments" or "Maybe the people in church are right. You ought to be more involved." Unwittingly he joins hands with the church — which only serves to isolate his wife. Now she feels as if both her husband and the church are against her.

One pastor with a failing marriage, who reluctantly agreed to attend Marble Retreat, was a high-energy worker who put in long hours not only in his parish but in the community. His wife had made it clear to him over and over that she was overwhelmed with the pressure of parish life. He considered his wife's distress a nuisance, and for years he acted as though it was her problem.

At Marble, his attitude didn't change. He insisted that he was right and that his wife had an assortment of failings and needed to make the adjustments. He might as well have stayed home: his judgmental attitude during the two weeks at Marble never softened. He stubbornly refused to take a hard look at what was fueling his wife's anger.

Undefensive Care

The most important thing to remember is this: if your wife resents you or the church, it isn't just her problem. It's yours as well — you certainly share in the consequences! Here are several principles that will go a long way towards making her problem yours and defusing her anger.

First, what a resentful wife needs most is to *feel* her husband's care about what's troubling her. One of the most common remarks I hear from pastors' wives is "I don't feel validated as a person; my feelings are not taken seriously." That's a legitimate complaint. Until your wife feels safe sharing unsafe feelings — without your becoming defensive — she will hold back. And that only reinforces the downward spiral.

That means you must make a risky move: ask her why she's angry and what *you* are doing to make things worse — a move not for lightweights.

Second, your wife needs your permission to be angry. She needs to feel supported and be given ample time to resolve her hurts.

Dirk was a typical pastor, eager to please, and he tried hard to be sensitive to his congregation. He could see their faults as much as his wife, Dara, did. It just seemed easier for him to overlook their insults. He figured a pastor and his wife had to be thick skinned.

Unfortunately Dara was more a doe than a rhino. She was emotionally fragile, and every barb wounded her deeply. Dirk was able to soothe her hurt, but when the hurt became resentment and then turned into bitterness and then blatant anger, he felt helpless.

He got scared when she blew her top about somebody at church. His fear erased his compassion. He tried to put a lid on her hostility. He was sure if he let her rage she would get out of control and destroy his ministry.

Regrettably his sharp, demanding tone only added to her feeling abused. Rather than help her control herself, his anger compounded hers. She stuffed her feelings down as long as she could. Then she totally blew up in a congregational meeting. His worst fear was realized.

As they worked through the conflict in counseling, Dara was finally able to explain to Dirk how she felt. She simply needed the freedom to express her anger in a safe place — at home with him. His clamping down on her had only thrown gas on an open flame.

Since a wife's resentment has most likely built up over time, time is what she needs most. Once you have communicated to her that you want to be part of the solution, I'd recommend occasionally asking, "How are you feeling about So-and-so?" Your question lets her know she hasn't been forgotten.

Third, encourage her to find support outside the church. It could be a friend, a support group, or a professional counselor. Of course, you'll need to be careful about recommending professional help. You don't want to communicate, "I need to send you somewhere to get fixed so you won't be such a drain on me and my ministry."

The best thing you can do is support her when *she* brings up the subject of getting outside help. If she does, give her your 100 percent support. Even if it means going to the church board to get money for her to do so. Many clergy couples are reluctant to let church leadership know of their struggles. Being careful about what you share is wise, but sometimes the need to get help outweighs the risk of revelation. Many pastors are surprised to find their church leaders supportive.

Finally, your wife needs to feel that, if push came to shove, she is number one to you, that, if need be, you would willingly leave the church on her behalf.

Scripture commands us to love our wives as Christ loved the church: he gave himself up for her. Would you be willing to resign for the sake of your marriage? Taking that verse seriously is a scary prospect.

I think the hardest thing I've ever given up for Melissa was my golf habit. I had to agree that two or three rounds of golf a week had become excessive. I don't know what I would do if she wanted me to quit psychiatry. I would like to believe I would go that far if she insisted.

So I have profound respect for Rick. His wife, Joan, didn't marry him when he was a pastor, and she was resistant to his leaving his secular job to enter seminary. Almost from the first day of his new career, she was unhappy. When he took his first church, her despondency grew. After a few distressing years, Rick could see that Joan wasn't able to adjust. She was a shy, private person and felt invaded by ministry demands. Rick bravely resigned and went back into his previous profession. He later told me it was the best move he had ever made.

The older I get, the less idealistic I am. Some conflicts cannot be resolved. Sometimes hard work and prayer just aren't enough. When your wife resents the church, the time may come to wipe the dust off your sandals and move to a new church. When your wife's hurt is too deep to stay where you are, your marriage must take center stage.

That's a painful decision. Here are a few questions to ask when wrestling with the decision to stay or move: If you stay in your church, what will be the effects on your wife? A nervous breakdown? Physical problems? In light of your wife's hostility, how effective do you feel your ministry can be? Is staying worth the price of possibly losing your marriage?

One caveat if you do move: any underlying problems in your marriage that created the need for a church transition need to be dealt with. If not, you will take those problems into the next church or your next phase of life.

Preempting Resentment

Conflict seems to be a regular part of life — in and out of the church. Yet the church environment is peculiar. Resentment flourishes in its soil. Here are three suggestions to keep it from taking root in your marriage.

• *Remember the little things.* One day in a group counseling session at Marble, with his wife sitting on the couch next to him, a pastor recalled an incident when his wife's behavior baffled him. It happened on Valentine's Day, which that year fell on a Sunday. Before heading off to church, he handed his wife a corsage. She was appreciative at the time, but later that afternoon, she became guarded, reserved, and distant.

"Tell the rest of the story," his wife interjected.

"The rest of the story?" he said. "What story?"

"I went to church that morning," she said, "and all the old ladies in the church had on the same corsage he had given me!"

Doing the special things, without taking shortcuts, can kill a lot of resentments.

• *Agree on how much to share with your wife.* Let's say one afternoon an elder walks into your office and unfairly lambastes you. You leave the office angry, but on the way home you question whether you should tell your wife about this incident. She is already peeved at this elder. Telling her might make her more angry than you are. What should you do?

I urge couples to decide, beforehand, how much should be shared. Some wives feel abandoned or neglected if their husbands don't give them the latest scoop: "I want to know. It makes me feel important, included, and loved when my husband lets me inside his head." Others would rather not be bothered; it only complicates life and colors their views of people in the church.

Before conflict arises, then, the pastor should ask his wife, "How do you feel about my sharing what is going on in the church? Is it better for you if I don't give you a play-by-play? Or would you prefer to know?"

● *Mitigate the pressures.* One pastor, when someone in his church would say, "We need cookies for next Sunday evening's gathering. Would your wife be willing to make those?" would respond, "I don't know. You'll have to talk to her." He let his wife be her own person. His response went a long way towards protecting his wife from undue pressure — and preempted resentment build-up.

Another pressure is money. Clergy are notoriously underpaid, and the burden of that largely falls on the spouse. She can't afford to dress her family as nice as other church families. The car she drives is more likely to be a dented 1984 Buick than a new Nissan Infiniti. Nor can she get her hair fixed as often as she would like. Always being strapped for cash makes her feel like a second-class citizen. Over time, it wears thin and can cause resentment.

This is a pressure point pastors should aggressively seek to relieve. That may mean being up-front with the church leadership about your salary shortfall: "We're just not able to make ends meet on my salary. Here's our budget."

Many, though, cower at the thought: *It might jeopardize my job. It might draw fire from the power brokers in the church.* But speaking up speaks volumes to your wife about your commitment to make your marriage work.

In the end, Travis and Barb, the couple in the opening story, survived Barb's resentment. After two weeks at Marble, where Barb worked on her anger and Travis assumed his responsibility for their struggles, they returned home knowing what they needed to do.

Together Travis and Barb met with the elders, and Barb told them how she had been feeling, how hurt she was, how she felt they had treated her and Travis unfairly. Remarkably, the elders listened, even acknowledging some of the hurt they had caused. Barb's anger was released, and she was reconciled to Travis and the church.

The explosive natural gas of resentment can be dispersed — if it is faced head on. Concerned, considerate pastors can make the church a reasonably safe place for their spouse to call home.

PART THREE
The Culture
and the Pastor

When it comes to people's expectations of the pastor, it's better to promise less and deliver more.

— Ed Dobson

CHAPTER EIGHT

Pushed to Be Omni-Competent

I knew a pastor of a large church who tried to control all aspects of his church. He worked seventy and eighty hours a week: he preached, did all the visitation, oversaw the staff, and micromanaged virtually every detail of the church's ministry.

I met with him from time to time over the course of a year and a half. He always had the same complaint, "I'm tired. I'm worn out. There is something flawed about ministry in a megachurch setting. It shouldn't be like this." I was saddened, but not surprised, when I learned that he had fallen into serious sin that cost him his ministry.

In spite of his fatigue, his impatience with others, his constantly being behind, his feeling of distance from God, he had been insistent on remaining in control of all aspects of the church's ministry. Why? Part of it, no doubt, was a result of his own psychological needs.

But a large part of it was due to modern church culture, the same culture that pressures all pastors. Over the last few decades, the expectations of congregations have been raised enormously. Whereas earlier we were expected to study, preach, and visit, now we're supposed to administer a variety of programs, raise enormous funds for larger and larger facilities, and counsel people with problems a previous generation never even heard of — all the while preaching as good as the latest televangelist.

Most pastors go into the pastorate with dreams of being able to do it all. That dream matches perfectly with the increasing demands of the congregation. The pastor, though, discovers quickly that he or she can't do it all. The expectations to keep up the image of the omni-competent pastor are so strong, it seems impossible to lower the expectations to reasonable levels, at least without appearing lazy.

But if you don't figure out a way to minister with realistic expectations, you will burn out, or worse. So how shall we minister in this situation?

Getting Off on the Right Foot

If you are starting ministry, or beginning a new ministry, you are in the best position to do something about it. Though expectations can be changed later, it's easiest to set things right in the beginning. Here are some steps I found helpful as I took on the pastorate at Grand Rapids.

● *Learn what the people expect.* It's not too early, even during the search process, to begin the work of negotiating expectations.

That is why, against the search committee's advice, I insisted on a two-hour, open-and-free-wheeling, question-and-answer session during my candidating weekend. The leadership feared it would open a can of worms.

"Who cares?" was my response. "Let's go ahead and open it and take a good look at the worms." I wanted to know what the hot buttons were and let the congregation see how I would handle sensitive and potentially divisive issues.

The session turned out to be wonderfully informative. I was asked about such issues as women in ministry, my position on divorce, and even what I thought about eating in a restaurant on Sundays (the so-called "Dutch laws" of the region look down on this).

Soon we were discussing people's expectations of their pastor. I was asked about my pastoral strengths and weaknesses, and my willingness to work with a strong board. Someone even wanted to know if I intended to start a Moral Majority chapter at the church.

This is not the only time or the only format available to us to discover what people expect of us. That we seek to discover what, in fact, people expect is the important thing. We don't want to be guessing.

● *Know what the board expects.* I had just begun my ministry at Calvary Church when a group approached me and asked that I become heavily involved in their particular program. When I met with the board, I told them of the request and said, "I'm uneasy about getting drawn into this, but I don't want to disappoint these people."

The chairman of the board immediately spoke up: "Pastor, the only people you have to worry about disappointing is us." We all laughed, yet he was making a serious point. Various factions in the congregation will attempt to place different expectations on your time and involvement, but what really matters is knowing what the board expects of you. They are the group you are answerable to month by month, even in a congregational polity.

That board member's remark led to a lengthy discussion regarding the use of my time. At the end, the board unanimously directed me to spend at least two-and-a-half days a week in study. I later announced that decision to the congregation, and from time to time I remind them of that board directive. That is one way of letting people know I can't be involved in everything.

● *Watch those promises.* The temptation begins in the interview process, but we never really shake it. We enter ministry because we want to help people. So we are regularly tempted to promise them more help than we can humanly deliver. Better to promise what we'll not do.

For example, early on in my ministry at Grand Rapids, I mentioned that I had never been a particularly good counselor: "I hope I'm a compassionate and sympathetic person. And if you come to see me, I'll listen and cry with you. But then I'll tell you to go home and read fifty chapters of the Bible and let God straighten out your problem! That is the limit of my understanding of counseling."

When it comes to people's expectations of the pastor, it's better to promise less and deliver more.

● *Set up a regular review.* Even though the board and I may have reached a mutual understanding regarding expectations, I still meet regularly with my chairman. It's part of an ongoing effort to remain on the same page with my leaders.

I also go through an annual review process with the board chairman, vice-chairman, and chairman of the deacon board. We look at the past year and discuss issues they feel I should pay attention to. If conflicts and differences are stirring, this gives us the opportunity to bring them out in the open and resolve them.

That can be a threatening process. If not handled with love and mutual respect, it can leave a pastor deeply wounded. My father pastored a church where the entire congregation voted yearly whether to retain him or let him go. It was a difficult, humiliating process to be subjected to.

But this has worked in my situation, and it has fostered regular communication about what people expect of me and what I can realistically do.

Getting Chips for Doing Your Thing

Leith Anderson once compared the ministry to a poker game. When you first arrive at a church, you're given a stack of chips. If you preach well, love the people, and see some successes, you're given more chips.

If you do something poorly or irresponsibly, you lose chips in a hurry. If you lose too many, you're thrown out of the game completely. But as you build trust with your board, they will over time give you more and more latitude in the exercise of ministry.

During my last review, after seven-and-a-half years of ministry, the board let me know it was unnecessary to check with each committee and board before I made a significant decision.

"You have the freedom to make choices on your own," they said. "All we ask is that you keep us informed."

The same trust works in regard to the congregation's expectations of the pastor. If year by year they see I've been a faithful pastor with my main responsibilities, they will be forgiving of areas they wish I could cover but cannot.

So, regardless of how many years you minister in a place, it's vital to work on the trust factor. There are many ways to establish or re-establish trust, but here are five that have worked for me.

First, I let people know I work hard. I once received this piece of advice from an old mountain preacher: "Son, whatever else you do, make sure people see you working. Park your car in front of the church so people can see it on their way to work in the morning. Then, if you like, go fishing for the day. But just make sure your car is parked in front of the church by the time people head for home!"

That humorous advice should be taken seriously. People have no idea how we spend our time, so we need to let them know that we do put in more than a few hours on the weekend. Once they recognize that, they are less apt to pile more expectations on our already busy schedules.

That's why one of my first edicts as senior pastor was to establish regular office hours for the staff and me. I let people know we would be in the office, putting in a full week's work. Because it's common knowledge that, in addition to holding regular office hours, I preach on Saturday night, three times on Sunday morning, and once on Sunday evening, people understand I don't have much time left to take on new obligations.

Second, I've also learned how to get things done without

doing them myself. When I planted a church in the mountains of Virginia, I had to do everything. I opened the doors, cleaned the church, answered the phone, ran the mimeograph machine, worked with the Sunday school teachers, helped lead the choir, and in my spare time, did all the preaching and visitation. All those things needed doing, and those were the things a pastor of a small church did.

I soon realized, though, that I shouldn't do all those things. So I found people to unlock the doors. I called on people to lead music and work with the Sunday school. I discovered that in a lot of cases, people don't care who does the job as long as it gets done. And when things get done, even if not done by me, people tend to give me more trust and leeway to do the things I think I should be doing.

Third, I have to be willing to meet some expectations that lie outside my areas of specialty. Though I'm not a natural counselor, as a pastor I still have to meet with people going through a divorce and with those struggling with substance abuse. Counseling comes with the pastoral territory. The congregation is right to expect me to fulfill this function at least to some degree. If I completely shirk the essential pastoral functions, I can be sure people will start questioning how I spend my time.

Fourth, when it comes to functions I think are essential to my ministry, it's imperative I do whatever it takes to do them with excellence. I can't rest on my laurels.

For example, even though preaching is one of my strengths, I devoted one year recently to read and study everything I could find about preaching. If a congregation sees me constantly growing in an area I say is important, they will give me more leeway to work in that area.

Finally, I've learned the art of symbolic gestures. For example, Calvary Church has always had a strong missions emphasis. Though I'm committed to missions, we have other pastors on staff who are called to give more attention to it. Still, I knew I needed to show the congregation that I thought this was a vital ministry.

So I decided that once a year I would visit mission fields, meeting with the men and women our church supports, in places like Haiti and Poland. Once I began doing that, people saw in a dramatic way that, although I wasn't on the front lines of administration and fund raising for missions, I did care about them.

Other pastors periodically visit each of the committees of the church, even though they don't plan to attend them regularly. Such a gesture communicates the pastor thinks each committee's ministry is important. And that alone often satisfies people's expectations in terms of your involvement.

Just Say, "No!"

No matter how much trust building you do in ministry, sometimes you simply have to refuse to meet people's unreasonable expectations.

Ray Ortlund once observed that every three or four years, regardless of how long you've been the pastor, some person or group in the church will inevitably challenge your leadership. It may come from the board, a staff member, or an element of the congregation. But someone is going to launch a direct attack concerning what is expected of you. Ortlund advises we dare not ignore it.

I faced such a challenge when we decided to begin another building program. Up until then, we had agreed that I was not expected to be the chief fund raiser in the church. In fact, when I first arrived, people were deeply concerned I would be too aggressive in raising money (they knew I had been mentored by Jerry Falwell).

My conviction has always been that if you preach the Bible and win people to Christ, God will take care of money. So that was the way I operated at Calvary. That worked fine until we entered a $5 million building program.

We agreed to ask people to make three-year pledges to the building fund. We decided that if we didn't receive the pledge amounts we needed, we wouldn't build.

Little by little as the campaign proceeded, and as anxiety rose about whether we would meet the goal, I began to feel the subtle pressure to become more assertive in fund raising. I knew several people were quietly thinking, *How could Dobson have spent all those years with Falwell and be so lousy at asking for money?*

At the end of the pledge drive, we had raised only half the target goal.

That is when I felt the pressure more than ever. Several members of the board thought I should go back to the congregation and make a pitch for the remaining money.

"I won't do that," I told the board. "We agreed that if we didn't raise the money we expected, we would stop there. Perhaps God is trying to tell us something. I suggest we put the project on hold for six months."

My position disturbed many people. I probably aggravated them further when I confessed to the congregation that we as a board didn't know just what to do next! I suggested that as a body we should wait and pray for direction.

Six months later the project was approved again by the congregation. This time the needed funds flowed in and eventually the first cement was poured.

And I never had to become a fund raiser.

Certainly the most important trait to nurture in working with a congregation is a submissive spirit. That has not always been easy for me. But sometimes I have to be submissive to people's reasonable expectations, even if I don't feel gifted or interested in a particular ministry. And sometimes I have to be submissive to God and pointedly inform the congregation that I can't do what they ask.

In either case, when I'm able to have a submissive spirit, my motive is love and a desire to serve. And few congregations expect more than that.

No one escapes the grip of personal insecurity. It's part and parcel of life after the Fall. The problem comes when our personal insecurities significantly affect our behavior.

— Louis McBurney

CHAPTER NINE

R–E–S–P–E–C–T

Over twenty years ago, I pulled out of mainstream psychiatry to start a counseling retreat for pastors. I still attend psychiatry seminars, and invariably someone will ask, "What do you do?" When I attempt to describe my present calling, I receive a puzzled look. Then an awkward silence.

"Mmm," the person says. "How nice."

Other psychiatrists' respect shouldn't matter to me. But it does. I yearn for the approval of my peers. Intellectually I know my self-worth is established by God through what Christ did on the cross, that I've been created and redeemed by him. Yet it's difficult resting in God's unconditional love while holding down a job many people I admire don't respect.

In working with pastors, I've learned this is a common feeling among them. There are lots of reasons for this.

The social fragmenting of our culture has heightened their insecurity. More and more I hear pastors say, "I don't feel trained to cope with the things that confront me daily." These things include the complications of blended families, sexual abuse, and marital breakup. It's hard to feel good about what you do when you're not sure what you're supposed to be doing.

Furthermore, the media portray the average pastor as a balding fiftysomething with a reversed collar and a paunch; sometimes the reverend is benignly kind; sometimes he's a hypocrite, but in any case, he's hopelessly out of touch with the "real world."

Nor do pastors get an emotional boost by comparing their work to other jobs requiring comparable education and having similar demands. Salaries seem painfully higher in law, in educational administration, and in business.

Finally, while our culture gives increasing status to specialists — pediatric ophthalmologists, nuclear medicine technicians, and bioelectrical engineers — pastors remain generalists. Like the family doctor, they seem to be a thing of the past. This is particularly unnerving for generalist pastors as they watch some churches become staffed with specialists.

Take Frank, for example, a "utility" pastor loaded with talent. He entered the playing field of Trinity Church. During his fifteen years there, he bounced from responsibility to responsibility, plugging in where needed. He was a generalist, and the church needed a generalist then.

His last five years at Trinity, however, the church exploded numerically. Increasingly the board was filled with leaders of industry, and Trinity was rapidly becoming a multi-staff church of specialists: a junior high pastor, a children's pastor, a small group pastor. Suddenly, Frank was a dinosaur, a low-tech pastor in a high-tech church. An outside consultant hired by the board said

Frank had to go, so Frank was terminated. In his place were hired four specialists.

A Tough Place to Work

Sometimes it's not broad social forces that aggravate our self-doubts but specific pastoral experiences. Unfortunately, the church can be a cruel place to work.

Dan, a pastor, felt good when he was courted by Long Valley Community Church for the second time. Nothing like a church approaching you to make you feel important. Though he had turned down the first offer, he was ready when the second came his way. He looked forward to pastoring a church that seemed to like him so much.

Soon after he arrived, however, dark clouds began clustering on the horizon. None of the church's power brokers was on the search committee, and they were not happy with Dan's innovative style (the reason the committee so vigorously pursued him). His attempt to rearrange the order of worship, for example, was met with stiff resistance. The typical grumbling turned into a roar: he was openly criticized at board meetings and in letters from members of the congregation.

Naturally, Dan began to doubt himself and his abilities. But rather than dealing with the criticism or facing his self-doubts, he simply withdrew. His office became a sanctuary. There he spent most of his days, studying for Sundays and programming the church computer. His relationships with the congregation grew colder and colder.

Determined to be heard, the opposition grew louder and louder. The disenfranchised part of the church elected to the elder board their turn-around man: a hard-nosed businessman "who would let the axe fall if needed." The first item on his agenda: send Dan to Marble Retreat to "get fixed."

When Dan arrived, his self-esteem sagged badly. As I alluded to in another chapter, when I learned of the dynamics surrounding his coming, I phoned the church chairman to satisfy myself that this wasn't merely a prelude to Dan's being fired, which is often the case. "If you expect Dan to get fixed instantly and come back a different person, you'll be disappointed. If sending him here is only a token stab at resolving the issues so you can say you've done everything you could before you fire him, I need to know. Then we'll spend the rest of his time here helping him work through the transition of leaving the church."

"No, no," the chairman replied. "All we want to do is help. He's our main concern; he's valuable to us. We wouldn't make any decision about his leaving for at least another year."

Two weeks after returning to his church, though, Dan was fired. If that wasn't enough, the chairman then warned him that if Dan so much as breathed a word of his termination, never again would he pastor in that denomination.

You can imagine Dan's psychological state at that point. Certainly, his is a worst-case scenario. But many pastors are treated cruelly by their churches, and that can have a devastating effect on their sense of self-respect.

The Face in the Mirror

Although the pummeling of the world and the church aggravate the problem of a pastor's self-respect, I believe the main issues lie deeper. Our doubts about our calling and our feelings of inadequacy are rooted in a poor self-image.

But let's face it: no one escapes the grip of personal insecurity. It's part and parcel of life after the Fall. The problem comes when our personal insecurities significantly affect our behavior. Here are several indications of insecurity gone haywire.

1. Compromised integrity. Each of us holds to convictions that shape who we are. From time to time, we question those convictions. That's all part of growing morally. But when we find ourselves wrestling time and again with basic issues, when we're not sure what is right and what is wrong, when we're afraid of making an ethical blunder but don't know what exactly we should do — that's when we should take a look at the issue of self-esteem.

For example, the male pastor who thinks he should caress the lonely divorcé to give her comfort is a confused pastor. He probably is lonely and unappreciated himself, and he has lost some ethical judgment in trying to compensate.

2. *Inflexibility.* When people don't respect us, we're tempted to *make* them respect us. So some pastors try to command respect by becoming more demanding. They overload their associates with work and then criticize them severely for not meeting deadlines. And they justify it by saying, "I'm no harder on others than I am on myself."

At board meetings, they refuse to budge on issues, even minor ones. "I can't let them push me around. If they won't let me purchase a new word-processing program to prepare my sermons, they won't respect me on vital issues." Such pastors end up making major issues out of minor ones, which all become "symptomatic of deeper issues."

3. *Physical symptoms.* When self-esteem sags deeply, it can show itself physically: panic attacks, insomnia, lack of appetite, depression. Almost any body system can be affected.

4. *Drivenness.* This is probably the most common symptom, the others often being aspects of this one.

For men in particular, the need to achieve, to invest tremendous energy into their work, is at least one part biological. Males are endowed with large amounts of testosterone, an anabolic chemical. The male body turns out large amounts of energy, which naturally gets channeled into work.

Striving to achieve outward success can be — but is not always — a symptom of deep-seated insecurity. A workaholic pastor may be attempting, say, to gain approval from his dead father who never affirmed him. Or he might be bolstering his weak self-image by being outwardly successful.

The driven person, rather than finding satisfaction in the work itself, needs a scorecard. He constantly compares himself with others. Rather than feeling satisfied and celebrating reaching a goal, he feels empty and guilty at what he has yet to accomplish.

A model for the way we should feel about our work comes from children. In his book *Your Pastor's Problems* (Augsburg, 1966), William Hulme says, "Jesus pointed to a child as the expression of human greatness. . . . The light touch of the child is an expression of his childlike faith. His enjoyment of his father's world is inseparable from his security in his father's world.

"Childhood, therefore, is not only something we go from but something we go toward. Enjoyment is probably closer to whatever we mean by human perfection than accomplishment. And anxiety over accomplishment may be the most telltale symptom of idolatry."

While learning to walk, our granddaughter would pull herself up and stand alone on wobbly legs. Seeing our smiles, she would shake her head and squeal with delight. Her grandparents squealed along with her. Her freedom and joy as she explored her new mobility, as she discovered her ever-expanding world, was as pristine as a blanket of new snow.

Driven people know little of this joy, the pleasure of expending oneself in God's creation, the satisfaction of discovering new worlds. They know only the ravenous need to achieve. And it all comes back to a basic need: to know one is already esteemed.

Realigning the Image

Whether a pastor's self-esteem is radically shaken or just in need of fine-tuning, his or her self-view needs to be regularly aligned with Christ's view. Here are three suggestions that may help.

● *Examine your calling.* Some pastors choose to go into ministry for the prestige or power that church leadership promises. Others see local church ministry as a safe place to have a career: "The pay may not be great but at least there people will like me." Still others, because of guilt, are hoping to work out their salvation: they feel they've never measured up, so they think, *Perhaps I can serve enough to compensate for what I've done or be significant by doing something that really matters.*

Unfortunately, the church is not a warm, safe place to acquire power, be liked, or atone for sin. If you've been called into ministry by such motives, instead of by Christ, ministry is bound to undermine your self-confidence. It will constantly disappoint you and make you feel like a failure, when in fact you're just not in the right calling.

• *Go back to the roots.* Our childhood environment figures into our adult internal struggles. Some people survive childhood believing they're okay no matter what they do. The majority of us, however, enter adulthood attempting to compensate for feeling negatively about ourselves. A major factor influencing our adult self-worth is our childhood family and peers.

I've counseled several pastors with learning disabilities. Growing up they weren't able to learn at the pace of their classmates. They were mocked and called derogatory names. One pastor told how in junior high school one of her teachers openly ridiculed her because she wasn't able to pronounce a word.

These incidents attach easily to our fragile psyche. Gather enough of them and soon we come to believe we're inferior, a no-good loser. Pinpointing the origin of our poor self-image goes a long way toward making changes. But it's not enough.

• *Reprogram your thinking.* This does not come naturally. What we've come to believe about ourselves over time is not easily erased. Yet it is possible.

In an earlier chapter, I told about the pastor who came to Marble feeling threatened about who he was. We talked at length about his childhood problems of acceptance and identity. The messages he had received from his parents growing up were mostly negative. His adult conversion had turned his life around, but he still agonized over his adequacy.

His two weeks at Marble were life changing. Besides him and his wife, three other couples there were working on their struggles as well. For two weeks, the four couples functioned as a support group. Each day the group met to talk about the common pressures of ministry and their effect on their lives. One of the discussion questions the group was asked to answer was simply "What's new?" By the end of that week, this pastor would reply, "What's new is *me.*" Finally he had begun to soak in the truth of his infinite worth in Christ.

Upon his return to the trenches, this pastor regularly used this question to reprogram his thinking about himself. When he caught himself saying, "I'm a failure," he would say, "What's new is me. I'm loved by God, who delights in me." He is still in process, but the change in him is real.

There is no magic wand for becoming more secure in Christ. It takes hard work, and even then, attacks of low self-esteem will likely hound us to the grave. But learning to rest in God's love is worth the journey. It instills in us a confidence to give to others even while feeling insecure.

Two Key Habits for Tough Settings

The root of our lack of confidence may be low self-esteem, but as I mentioned, this often gets aggravated by the environment in which we work. I give pastors who work in self-image-challenging settings a couple of habits to develop.

First, stick up for yourself. No one respects a doormat. If, for example, you feel pressured to produce beyond what you can physically handle, go to your elder board and say, "For me to continue to be effective as a pastor, I need to set limits on the number of things I'm responsible for around here. I'm finding I just can't get everything done. Let me give you some of my suggestions for dealing with this, and then I'd like to hear yours. I'd like us to come to a new agreement."

Instead of withdrawing into his office, if Dan had confronted those who complained about his changes in the worship service, explaining why he did what he did, enlisting their help in forming a vision for the church, he might have been able to short-circuit his eventual firing.

Second, work to be heard, not to be right. Truth can be presented one of two ways: with horsepower, which puts everyone on the defensive, or with tact and gentleness. Too often, especially in the church, truth is presented in a combative way. As a result, the messenger draws unnecessary fire, and the message is dismissed.

You don't have to shout or even be angry. Just a calm, simple, steady explanation is all that is usually necessary. Happily enough, once you respect yourself well enough to speak up for yourself, others gain greater respect for you as well.

In recent years, I've found myself concerned enough about several social issues to write letters to the local newspaper editor and to make public statements that were unpopular. This has taught me that even tough subjects can be handled peaceably. My community may not agree with what I say, but they heard my message. When I'm faced with delivering an unpopular opinion, I've learned to be more concerned about communication than conversion.

Ministry Goes On

I think it's fair to say Jesus encountered his share of disrespect. His troubles wound up getting him crucified. Yet while despised, put down by the media elite of his time, and even betrayed by his friends, he continued to serve. *That's easy for him,* we might think, *he never had the doubts and fears that I do.*

Maybe, maybe not. But I know that you don't have to wait for your self-image to be completely renewed before you minister to others. Otherwise we would never get around to ministry! Instead, even while grappling with these issues, you can be an effective pastor.

Years ago a pastor who attended Marble because of marital problems got divorced. It was his second. In his denomination, divorce didn't disqualify one from ministry, but after two failures, no church was knocking his door down to be their pastor.

The urban church that finally hired him was desperate; they were about to shut the place down. A few years earlier, they had built a new facility, saddling themselves with a large mortgage. Instead of growing, the church began losing members and consequently couldn't service the debt. Surveying the hopeless situation, the denomination essentially said to this pastor, "Give it a shot. See what you can do."

Though dogged by self-doubt and feeling like an outcast, this man went to pastor this dying church. His plan was simple: love the people. He did this by visiting everyone in the community who needed a pastor. When he learned a family had lost a child or a grandparent, or that someone was having problems, he would drop by the house and say, "I pastor one of the churches in the community. I know you must be going through some tough times. Is there anything I can do to help?" Because of his own doubts and struggles, he was able to empathize with others. Instead of the cheap answers he might have suggested earlier in his ministry, he simply offered only his presence and his ears.

Slowly the church began to awaken. Eventually it paid off its debt and even added an educational wing. Today the church is a thriving fellowship. Their pastor still has periodic battles with self-doubt, but in the meantime, while he is working to integrate Christ's love into his own life, he is loving his people as best he can.

And it seems to be enough.

Few people work under higher expectations to be nice than pastors, yet few occupations nurture as much anger.

— Ed Dobson

CHAPTER TEN

When Pastoring Makes You Angry

My father pastored in Belfast, Northern Ireland, for seven years. Every Sunday he preached and then walked to the door to shake parishioners' hands. And every Sunday one man said on his way out, "Well, you got it off your chest again, didn't you?"

I never heard my father complain about that man's disrespect for his preaching (he only recently told me about it). He was able to forbear.

If the same thing happened to me, I would probably go to that man, ask him what his problem is, and suggest there are 480

Protestant churches in town, one of which should be able to please him!

Pastoral life is ripe soil for rage. Criticism comes often and unfairly. Hard work may return small tangible results. Members resist leadership and change. Conflicts among church workers are endemic. Volunteers don't show up for promised work. We're pulled between giving our best to our families or to the church. There is never enough money, never enough time, never enough help. The work is never done.

Few people work under higher expectations to be nice than pastors, yet few occupations nurture as much anger. The result: many pastors are like a wide spot in a swiftly flowing river. On the surface, the water is fairly placid, but underneath is a dangerous undercurrent.

What should we do about this undertow of frustration, hurts, aggravation?

Recognizing the Anger

In our culture, many people think of the pastor as the nicest person in town, always smiling as benignly as a funeral director, never offended by even the unkindest cut. Consciously or unconsciously, most pastors try to live up to the omni-nice image.

That is as it should be; we are to be forbearing. The problem comes when we're so afraid of getting angry that we cannot recognize when we are. And that seems to be the case with many pastors; they just don't recognize how angry they are.

Many deny it or cloak it with euphemisms, but anger shows up: break downs in communication (not returning phone calls, for example), withdrawal from relationships (cocooning in the office), depression, even heightened sexual temptation. Three signs in particular seem most common:

● *Sarcasm.* What we fear to say in seriousness we sometimes joke about. A pastor who is resentful of the power of the women's group might during announcements say, with a smile, "This Friday night, there will be a meeting of the real board in our church — the women's group!" Everyone laughs, but this is not good-natured humor. It is sarcasm, and sarcasm cuts.

● *Impatience at home.* A pastor is hurt and angry at the members of the board, but he doesn't say anything. Week after week at church, even as he speaks with members of the board, he keeps a warm smile on his face. At board meetings, he calmly accepts criticisms. Church members comment about their sweet, godly pastor.

But at the pastor's home, it's another story. When his wife serves dinner late, this pastor explodes. He rarely plays with his children, and when he does, he snaps at them repeatedly. He slams doors and is rude to telephone salespeople.

At home he feels out of control, and he wonders why he can't be more patient. Or he explains it away: "I've just had a hard day." But the fact that this behavior repeats itself signals that something deeper is going on.

● *Preaching about "them."* I pity sinners in the hands of an angry preacher.

One pastor I know was preaching through the Book of Philippians at a time when a faction in the church was causing him a lot of problems. One Sunday the text in Philippians spoke directly to what the pastor saw as the attitude problems of his opposition. In his sermon, when he spoke to those verses, he couldn't resist talking about the "people in churches who are like this" and how they destroy churches.

He didn't name names, and he was careful not to look at any of the dissenters, but at that point in the sermon, he spoke with extraordinary fervor — what he now sees as anger. He spoke about "these people" with apocalyptic tones and without grace, as if they were demons. Everyone aware of the problems knew whom the pastor was talking about.

Of course, this veiled attack only strengthened the dissenters' opposition. Months later, when they handed him a four-page letter chronicling their complaints, one item was his "using the pulpit to attack people in the church."

Because anger is so difficult to recognize, I have asked my wife and other church leaders to be warning lights for me. I have given them permission to tell me when they suspect I'm chronically angry or to ask, "Ed, are you angry about this?"

If you drive by a waste dump, you will likely see several pipes sticking from the ground with a large flame burning at the top. As buried garbage decomposes, it emits methane gas. Pipes are buried throughout a waste dump to siphon off the methane and burn it safely. Otherwise, periodically, as the methane gases build up, the dump could explode in flames.

Burying anger and pretending it's not there is similarly dangerous. Recognizing it is discomforting, but it's the first step in healing.

Putting a Nice Face on Rage

If we don't directly deny the anger, we may try to put a nice face on it. We recognize the powerful emotion, but we call it something good.

I can, for instance, describe myself as "a person of conviction" outraged by sin around me. I have listened to many sermons by angry preachers. Usually they call people ugly names, generalize, and overstate their case.

But prophets are not exempt from the calling to express the fruit of the Spirit: love, joy, peace, patience, kindness, goodness, faithfulness, gentleness, and self-control. The angry-prophet model, which you will have a hard time finding even in the Old Testament, is clearly not the pattern for New Testament pastors: "The Lord's servant must not quarrel; instead, he must be kind to everyone, able to teach, not resentful. Those who oppose him he must gently instruct, in the hope that God will grant them repentance leading them to a knowledge of the truth" (2 Tim. 2:24, 25).

Some people point to Jesus to justify preaching out of anger. But when Christ rebuked people, as he does in Matthew 23 in a series of woes, it was usually against hypocritical religious leaders and self-righteous legalists. I don't often have an opportunity to preach to such people; mostly I'm speaking to lay people, people trapped in their sins. So usually "prophetic anger" doesn't have much of a place in the pulpit.

We may rationalize anger by saying we are identifying with

the poor and oppressed; we are giving voice to the victim's rage, showing we understand the pain of the exploited.

Fortunately, there are better ways to identify with the oppressed. Prayer is perhaps the most effective. On Mother's Day, for example, people are seated before me who grew up in broken homes or who were abused by their mothers. There are singles who were abandoned or divorced by their spouses and are struggling to provide for their children.

On such a day, a lot of hurt and anger resides in the congregation. So I try to express that yet without anger. In my pastoral prayer, I'll say, "Lord, you know the pain and anger these people feel. I cannot honestly say that I know how they feel; I have never gone through what they have endured. But you know, and I ask you to extend special grace and comfort to them this day."

Some pastors say, "I'm angry because that's who I am. I'm being real. Not to express my anger is to pretend to be something I'm not."

Then again, there is more to life than being genuine. Sometimes kindness and maturity demands that we put aside anger for the time being.

Finally, some pastors rationalize their anger by claiming it enables them to lead a group effectively. "If you're going to be the leader," it is argued, "once in a while you better stand up and let the board have it."

Such outbursts keep people at a distance, and in one sense earn respect, but it's the wrong kind of respect. People avoid crossing angry pastors because they fear their temper, not because they respect their leadership. In the long run, you are much better served by putting your foot down only on weighty issues and doing so with gentleness.

Calming the Storm

When Scripture encourages us not to let the sun go down on our anger, it implies that we can do something healthy with it. Here are three ways I deal with anger.

1. Talk about it. When I first came to Grand Rapids, I asked one of the staff members to take care of an issue. Several days later, I asked if he had followed through on it.

"No," he said. "I didn't think it was a good idea."

I was so angry, I didn't say anything. For weeks, rather than ask him to do things I felt were his responsibility, I took care of them myself.

Finally, I went to him and told him I was shocked that he hadn't done what I had asked. I told him that if he thought my ideas were not good to tell me rather than ignoring me. Today, we laugh about the incident.

Most of us hate confrontation. I know I do, and anyone who does not probably wouldn't make a good pastor. But if someone is violating biblical principles, we will have to say something.

The injunction of Matthew 18 to go to those who sin against us just makes good sense. As poet William Blake put it,

I was angry with my friend;
I told my wrath, my wrath did end.
I was angry with my foe;
I told it not, my wrath did grow.

Of course, we can't confront people over every little offense. Pettiness and defensiveness are wearisome. We need time to process what has happened so we don't confront others under the sway of pain and emotion or over a matter that was simply a misunderstanding. We need time to think through what the issue is and how and when we are going to deal with it.

I confront someone only when my feelings are under control. Anger is unsettling and frightening to others. So I prefer to say they "hurt" or "disappointed" me. But in general I try to talk about the issue, not my emotions.

● *Count to a million.* Much of the time, we are called to forbear what angers us.

I now and then catch wind of an uncomplimentary comment made about me. My tendency is to assume the worst. If it seems serious enough, I call individuals about what they have said. When we talk it out, I usually discover that things have been blown out of proportion, and that clears things up.

Several years ago, as I preached in a southern church, I read from the NIV Bible; I had forgotten that this congregation was a strong supporter of the KJV. Weeks later I heard that the pastor of that church was angry with me. He reportedly had told several staff members that I was arrogant, insensitive, and foolish, and that I would never preach in his pulpit again. I got the impression this man was furious with me.

So I called him and then went to visit him. He had been bothered by what I had done, but he said he was hardly furious. We managed to resolve the issue.

Such experiences have taught me to take negative comments with a grain of salt, being patient as much as possible. I do admire the forbearance of my father, who pastored in the generation when ministers believed they should always accept abuse as lambs mutely going to slaughter. Although I never heard him say anything negative about people in church or about ministry, I now know that he was misrepresented, abused, and taken advantage of. He was hurt many times, but he never struck back.

While there are times we need to confront those who seriously hurt us — as much for their sakes and the church's sake as for our own — I think my father's example has a lot going for it. More often than not, I want to bear the nicks and cuts that are part of the pastoral terrain, to be "slow to anger," "not resentful."

Healthy forbearance (versus denial of anger) involves adopting an attitude of forgiveness, willingly embracing, for Christ's sake, the pain that others mete out to us.

• *Keep your balance.* A balanced life — including exercise, family time, and fun — helps me keep life's hurts in perspective. I run three to seven miles daily; after running four or five miles, my anger is often exercised right out of me.

I also try to get a good night's rest; for me that means at least seven-and-a-half hours. This regimen is essential for both my physical and emotional health. When I become tired or emotionally strung out, even small offenses become critical wounds.

Not Even the Appearance

If people perceive I'm angry, then the effect is about the same as if I were angry. So I've learned to be cautious in a couple of areas.

The first is flippant remarks. In my first year at this church, I preached a series on women in ministry. A few weeks before, I announced from the pulpit my plans to preach that series and then jokingly added, "Of course, it may be a two-minute series."

The following week I received a scathing letter from a female attorney in our congregation: "Every day in the marketplace, I struggle with what it means to be a woman, to be perceived as second class. Last Sunday a person I respect as godly made light of the problem."

I knew I had made a huge mistake. As far as I knew, I didn't have any anger toward women, and the purpose of my sermon series was to affirm women in ministry, but my hearers didn't know that. I knew I had to apologize to her.

Another area concerns preaching. One Sunday while preaching in Romans 1, I was talking about the sin of homosexual conduct. I noticed a man who had not been in church for several months. He was a homosexual, a married businessman living a double lifestyle. He had the HIV virus and had recently been so ill the doctors thought he would die.

I came to verse 27: "Men committed indecent acts with other men, and received in themselves the due penalty for their perversion." I thought, *Maybe I should skip this part today. It is this man's first day back in church. He's going to think I'm preaching at him.* But I quickly decided, *No, I'm obligated to preach the whole truth.*

At the same time, I knew I needed to speak the truth in love, otherwise this man might view me as just an angry moralist. So I made sure that I spent as much time on God's forgiveness as on his judgment.

Curing the Long Madness

"Anger is a short madness," said Horace. I would add that anger not dealt with biblically becomes a long madness. However we rationalize our wrath, the fact is anger "does not achieve the righteousness of God." That is true for several reasons.

First, anger is wedded to hostility. As lust is to adultery, anger is to murder. When we are angry, we usually have a desire to hurt.

Second, ironically, anger is impotent. Unleashing it doesn't solve anything but almost always adds fuel to destructive flames.

Third, anger cripples us. It limits our ability to model a Christlike life, which is the source of all long-term and effective ministry.

Fourth, anger is the mark of spiritual failure. In 1 Timothy and in Titus, most of the qualifications for ministry have something to do with self-control.

Instead, spiritual leadership requires that, as much as is possible, we short-circuit anger. And the only biblical way to do that is to forgive and to ask for forgiveness.

In one recent board meeting, I had some conflict with an individual. At the close of the meeting, I said, "Before we go, I need to apologize to Phil in front of everyone. I was abrupt and defensive in what I said. I don't want us to leave this meeting with that unresolved. Phil, I'm asking you to forgive me."

Phil forgave me on the spot. Asking forgiveness may not be the way it's done in the world, but it is Christ's way. It is one way we show the life-changing power of the gospel.

Intimacy is a feeling. Though we can't base our assurance of salvation on emotions, feeling close to God *is important.*

— *Wayne Gordon*

CHAPTER ELEVEN

Finding Time for God

Our church had met in a storefront for five years when we decided we needed more room. For several years, we had eyed the property across the street, a building that needed major remodeling. We offered $25,000 and finally settled on a price of $35,000.

Any mortgage would seriously tax our church budget, and the cost of remodeling still lay ahead. We needed to paint inside and out, erect walls for office space and classrooms, fix the roof, and lay new carpet. To save money I served as general contractor and carpenter. We were anxious to move in, so the remodeling was a high priority for the church and my daily schedule. After a quick morning devotion — a fast reading of a psalm and a "Bless me today, Lord!" — I rushed to the job site, where I hammered nails, called subcontractors, took estimates, and directed volunteers, often until eight o'clock at night.

Only after that, when I was done with the building project for the day, did I start my pastoral work: writing sermons, visiting in homes and at the hospital, and phoning leaders to plan services.

After a few weeks of this schedule, I paid the price. I wasn't just tired; my body screamed for rest. I felt emotionally distant from my wife and children, and they were obviously unhappy about not getting more of my time. Worst of all, I felt as though God was a star system away.

But I felt I *had* to finish the project soon. To reach the neighborhood as we had envisioned, with a medical clinic, gym, and larger facilities for Sunday services, we had to sacrifice. I kept telling myself, *I have to pay the price.* So I kept pushing.

Around that time, I bought *Ordering Your Private World* by Gordon MacDonald. (I didn't have the time to read, but I knew I needed help!) The book stopped me in my tracks. As I read one page in his book, I was sure MacDonald had been looking over my shoulder for the past several months:

"A driven person is usually caught in the uncontrolled pursuit of expansion. Driven people like to be a part of something that is getting bigger and more successful. . . . They rarely have any time to appreciate the achievements to date. . . .

"Driven people are usually abnormally busy. They are usually too busy for the pursuit of ordinary relationships in marriage, family, or friendship . . . not to speak of one with God."

The scales fell from my eyes. I had pursued the building project like someone who was driven not called. But that was only the symptom of a deeper problem.

I realized that I knew a lot about God — I had graduated from Wheaton College with a master's degree in Bible — but I didn't know God intimately. Like stars and planets in the night sky that I only occasionally lifted my head to wonder at, God was distant. I wasn't content with that. So in 1985, I launched out on a journey, a journey toward a deeper walk with God.

The Ways to Intimacy

Elder Christian statesmen like John Stott and John Perkins inspire me because they show that intimacy with God can keep growing throughout our lives, that greater intimacy is indeed a journey. Since that fall of 1985, I have gradually discovered a deepening sense of closeness with the Lord. Perhaps some of what I have learned can help you.

• *Follow your feelings.* Of course, pastors often must tell Christians not to follow their emotions (they are the caboose, and all that). But intimacy *is* a feeling. Though we can't base our assurance of salvation on emotions, *feeling* close to God is important. It makes our relationship with God fulfilling, and our faith, contagious.

What helps me feel closer to God? For years the mainstay of my daily devotions was Bible study. Although vital to true knowledge of God, Bible study doesn't normally foster intimacy for me. The key for me is waiting quietly on God until I sense his presence.

• *Get born again.* Bill Leslie, pastor of LaSalle Street Church in Chicago for several decades, felt burned out at one point in his ministry, so he went to a Catholic retreat center. He talked to a nun about how he felt. She listened patiently, and then she said, "What you need is a personal relationship with Jesus Christ."

Ouch! Bill was a card-carrying evangelical. That experience jarred him and convinced him he needed to deepen his relationship with the Savior.

Ministry is more than constructing buildings and leading people to Christ. It is knowing God and being the person he wants me to be. Out of that flows ministry. When asked what the greatest commandment was, Jesus didn't begin, "Love your neighbor as yourself." Rather, "Love the Lord your God with all your heart and with all your soul and with all your mind." I wasn't exempt from this command just because I was doing ministry. I needed to make first things first.

• *Follow the cycle of intimacy.* Knowing God is a process that can no more be exhausted than the exploration of the universe. There is always another blazing, star-saturated galaxy to discover in God.

John 14:21 describes the stages in the cycle: "Whoever has my commands and obeys them, he is the one who loves me. He who loves me will be loved by my Father, and I too will love him and show myself to him." Stage one: if we love God, we obey his commands. Stage two: if we obey his commands, he reveals himself to us. Stage three: when he reveals himself to us, we know him better and love him more. Then the cycle repeats itself, with our love and knowledge of God growing ever deeper and stronger.

Unless accompanied by obedience, prayer and Bible reading cannot bring intimacy. At one point in their history, the Israelites rigorously practiced spiritual disciplines. They were fasting, worshiping in the Temple, seeking the Lord. But God told them, in Isaiah 58, that he had another kind of fasting in mind. They needed to follow the spiritual discipline of obedience: to stop oppressing their workers, to feed the hungry and set prisoners free. God promised to come near those who obeyed him.

Of course, no one obeys perfectly, but deliberate, ongoing disobedience breaks the cycle of intimacy as surely as eating the apple sent Adam and Eve packing from the garden of Eden.

● *Journal first thoughts of the morning.* I am not a natural writer. Journaling is the last spiritual discipline I naturally gravitate toward. But a number of writers I had been reading recommended the practice, so I decided to try it.

I've never stopped. Ten years later I'm still journaling nearly every day. While the street lights are still shining bright on Ogden Avenue, I wake up, walk the cracked and vaulted sidewalks to church, crank up the footrest on my easy chair, and sloppily write in a spiral notebook things (unlike John Wesley) I never want anyone to read.

The thoughts I have when I wake, shower, and shave are the first thing I record in my journal. Early morning thoughts are significant. Worries, anger, new ideas, plans — they cluster at dawn, before the press of daily events, and in my journal I process them.

My journal is the one place where I can be completely honest with God.

Where I journal, pray, and read Scripture is important. On Saturdays I have tried to wake up early and journal at home, but even though I'm up before my family, it doesn't work. I don't get the same settled feeling in my spirit. I'm restless. Just as seeing a deep-space supernova is more likely if an astronomer is 7,200 feet above sea level at the Cerro Tololo observatory in Chile, so my best times with God come when I'm at my right place: my office.

● *Think twice about spiritual disciplines that upset family rhythms.* For one six-month period, I fasted one day a week. My family eats together every night, and so on fasting days I sat at the table and talked, but that was awkward. So I tried cloistering myself in the bedroom to read and pray during meals. "For a while I'm not going to eat with everyone on Mondays," I explained to the kids (trying not to sound super-spiritual). "While you're eating, I'm going to be alone with God because I want to know God better." My spiritual quarantine upset everyone. My wife was frustrated at having to handle the meal and children alone, and the kids wanted to see me.

After six months the fasting hadn't helped me feel significantly closer to God, but it had increased family stress. That spiritual discipline finally went out the window.

I still believe in the benefits of fasting (which I have since concluded benefits me most when I fast in three- to five-day stretches). Fasting over important decisions helps me stay focused. I have never come down from Mount Sinai with tablets in my hands, but I usually get a deep, settled peace.

I also fast about specific needs. When I taught high school, I met with another coach in the athletic equipment room during lunch hour; instead of eating, we prayed for the troubled marriage of a friend. After nine months, that marriage recovered.

My most refreshing spiritual discipline is keeping an agreement made with my wife years ago. We have promised each other to take a week away together every year with no children, no agenda; we want to simply enjoy each other. We pray and read the Bible together, rest, and play tennis. It is the highlight of our marriage and my spiritual life.

● *Get quiet and make time.* To have intimacy with God in my quiet time, I can't do without two things: (1) quiet, and (2) time.

As a student at Wheaton College, I was a fellowship fanatic. I love being with people. One year I went on a wilderness retreat. Retreat organizers told us to bring only three things beside our clothes and toiletries: a Bible, a notebook, and a pen. For three days they required that participants spend their time alone with God. I had never spent half a day away from people and alone with God! I quickly learned how dependent my relationship with God was on others. I also learned that spending quantity time with God enhances intimacy, and that I could enjoy the quiet and the luxury of time with God alone.

There is no substitute for time. I can't rush intimacy. When I have been away from my wife for several days, five minutes of conversation at the dinner table does not restore our sense of closeness. We need one or two hours together. What we discuss isn't as important as spending the time with each other.

I have a friend who talks about how much he enjoys "wasting time" with God, that is, spending unstructured, unhurried periods with the Lord. Although I often use a prayer list, I also like following no agenda, just as one of my favorite activities with family and friends is just hanging out together. Fellowship with God isn't rocket science. It has to be led by the Spirit and by the concerns and feelings on my heart at the moment.

In some of the most intimate moments my wife and I have shared, we haven't said anything; we sit or lie together holding hands or arm in arm, enjoying each other's presence. So it is with the Lord. "Be still, and know that I am God" is a verse that shapes my time with God as much as any other. Such stillness energizes me. Along with journaling, my greatest sense of closeness to God comes when sitting in silence before him until I feel his presence.

A Pastor's Disciplines Are Different

Bringing up the subject of "spiritual disciplines" usually brings up guilt in people. We all feel we could do more in this area. In addition, pastors are often troubled because they feel that the pressures of pastoral life encourage them to cheat God.

I believe, however, that we need to accept that our practice of spiritual disciplines will be different than the practice of our parishioners. In particular, there are three areas that trouble us, but here's how I deal with them.

First, I've come to accept that pastoral life is a ride on the Screaming Eagle. One day I'm ministering to a young man in prison for murdering a storekeeper; the next day I perform a wedding; the next day, a funeral. We can talk about balance and order, but pastoral life isn't balanced or ordered!

That means I've decided I'm not going to feel guilty when I have to miss a day of devotions. If I don't do them before 7 A.M., they don't happen, or at least they don't have the same benefit. When I can't fit in my quiet time, I feel cheated. I miss my time with the Lord. But if I am legalistic about spiritual disciplines, they no longer are *spiritual* disciplines for me, just mere duty.

Second, I merge daily devotions with sermon preparation. I know some consider that a problem, but it works well for me. I often read and meditate daily on my preaching text for the coming Sunday. My best preaching is a reflection of how I'm growing and what God shows me in my times with him.

Third, I allow myself to think about church during my quiet time. For some, this becomes a temptation to refuse to get personal with God, to keep playing pastor even in his presence. But I am a pastor, and so much of what I do is pastoral. Often as I wait in God's presence, ideas come like a meteor shower in my mind, and many are from the Lord: program ideas, insights into church problems, people to call. I write them down in full when the inspirations come and sometimes act on them immediately.

Recently as I was praying, the name of one woman in our church came to me. I wasn't sure why, but I sensed I was supposed to call her. When I did phone, she told me she had been struggling for several days. She desperately needed someone to talk to. She was shocked that I called just when I did.

Locking the Door

It's no surprise that my spiritual lows come when I'm busy, preoccupied, focusing my attention on everything but God, and my spiritual highs come on "sabbath" days of rest and relaxation. God instituted sabbath not only because the human body needs physical rest, but more so because human activity frustrates intimacy with the Creator.

That means that at times I've had to take forceful steps to make this happen.

As a people-person and activist, I've prided myself on having an open-door policy. So for years, people regularly interrupted my devotions, but it didn't bother me much. When I started my journey of knowing God, I knew something had to change; I had to find uninterrupted time with God. So I started coming to church earlier for my morning devotions.

Then people who wanted to see me learned a good time to catch me was early in the morning. Still, I kept my door open and kept coming in earlier and earlier to be alone.

One early morning as I was in my office praying, a drug addict named John, to whom I had been ministering for months, came to my door and said, "I don't have any money for the train. Can you give me a ride to work?"

"I'll give you some money," I said.

"I'll be late for work. I need you to give me a ride."

He pressed his plea, and so finally I drove him. When I returned to the office, I never was able to resume my devotions.

I woke early the next morning looking forward to my devotions. I settled into my chair at the office and began reading the Bible. Minutes later John showed up again at my door. Same request. Again I refused. He begged me, and once again I grudgingly interrupted my time with the Lord to drive him to work. Once again I couldn't resume my devotions later in the day.

The next morning, John reappeared at my open door. "I'm not driving you to work," I said firmly. "I have a commitment."

"Coach, you have to! I'll be fired if I don't get there on time."

"That's too bad. I have a commitment."

John pleaded and pleaded with me. Finally I said, "Okay, okay, I'll drive you to work, but if you come to my door tomorrow, I'm not driving you. You'll just have to lose your job."

The next morning I was not surprised when John stuck his head in my office (with that kind of persistence how could he not succeed in life!). But this time I held firm. Angrily he rushed out to take the train, and he didn't lose his job.

That experience seven years ago was a turning point for me. Though contrary to my nature, I started saying no to people to guard my time with the Lord. I now close and lock my outer office door during devotions. When someone knocks, I don't answer, nor do I answer my phone. I have told the congregation, "If you come knocking on my door early in the morning, I'm not going to answer. I need to be alone with God. I don't want to know *about* God, I want to *know* God."

Just a couple of years ago, I found myself deeply discouraged about the work at the church. Frankly, I debated quitting ministry at Lawndale. So, feeling like the despondent Elijah when Jezebel had designs on his prophetic skin, I went off by myself to a retreat. I fasted, prayed, and waited for three days to hear from God.

There were no temblors or bolts of lightning, but when the three days were up, the tide had come back in. I sensed God saying, *Be still. Know that I am God. You don't have to solve all of Lawndale's problems or save everyone you meet. Love me, and we'll work together. Just keep going.*

Returning home, I talked it over with my wife, and we decided to stay. We are now in our twentieth year of ministry at Lawndale Community Church. My eight-year journey in pursuit of intimacy with God is what enabled me to work through that dark night of my ministry. Often it is difficult to find time for God in the midst of church life, but closeness with God is the basis for lasting ministry.

*When there have been harrowing storms to weather in
ministry, the remembrance of God's original call to
me — to preach — is one thing that has helped me stick
to it.*

— Ed Dobson

CHAPTER TWELVE
Renewing Your Sense of Call

The week after Easter, I received this letter:

"This was [written] after considerable prayer. My husband
and I are submitting to the will of God and the urging of other
Christians by walking away from your church.

"While we could easily slip out unnoticed and certainly never
be missed, which is definitely one of the problems here, I feel that
our reasons for leaving are important enough to share with you.

"From the pulpit recently we heard you comment that there's
not enough unity between our church and other denominations.

This, Pastor Dobson, is ecumenism, and ecumenism is of the anti-Christ. . . .

"With which of these apostates would you suggest we unite? Our church in one broad sweep is trampling the grace of God and mocking the gospel. The church is the body of Christ, Pastor Dobson, not the unsaved masses of humanity you're trying to attract. Our church offers a program for every aspect of society that sets its foot in its walls — single moms, single dads, fatherless children, divorced women, substance abusers, but virtually nothing for believers.

"Although the church may be growing, you are losing the true saints of God. If this has been your goal, you are to be congratulated because you're achieving it. If not, there's still time to turn away."

It was signed, "In Christ, a saint."

At the bottom of the page, it read, "And thou, Capernaum, which are exalted in the heaven shall be brought down to hell. For if the mighty works which had been done in thee had been done in Sodom, it would have remained until this day. But I say to you it will be more tolerable for the land of Sodom in the day of judgment than for thee."

The same week I received another letter, a response to my sermon, "Smile; It's Easter and God Loves You."

The letter said, "Greetings. Visits to your church have left the following impressions. . . . [There was] a vapid, soft, and comfortable presentation on Easter with the emphasis on smile rather than our sinfulness driving the Suffering Servant to the Cross. This was so irreverent and out of place as to make one ashamed, not of the gospel, but of its hapless, harmless, one-sided view. . . . God help us. Whatever happened to the offense of the Cross?"

It was signed, "An Unhappy Camper."

After the high of Easter Sunday, this was not pleasant reading. Unfortunately, criticism is a regular part of Christian ministry. Sometimes it makes us wonder, "Is this job worth it?"

Add to those times in ministry when nothing seems to be happening, and we're sure it isn't worth it!

Now add to that our culture's presentation of clergy on TV,

movies, and in magazines — meek, mild, irrelevant, and out of touch with the "real" problems of the world — and one's very calling can be thrown into sudden and wrenching doubt: "Is ministry something I should be investing my life in?"

Yes, sometimes it's hard to remember why we're in ministry, or whether it's worth it. So periodically, we need to think about our call afresh.

Reviewing Your Sacred History

"My spirit grows faint within me," wrote David. "My heart within me is dismayed." So what does he do? "I remember the days of long ago, I meditate on all your works and consider what your hands have done" (Ps. 143:4–5).

This is how David renewed his own sense of call. It's not a bad idea for pastors to do the same from time to time — to remember what God has done in their lives and ministries.

I find it especially helpful to remember the origin of my call to ministry. I grew up in a pastor's home, so there were some subliminal expectations from church people that I would follow my father. Though my parents never pushed that agenda on me, others did, and I reacted to it. As far as I was concerned, it was none of their business what I did with my life.

I was 16 when I went away to a Bible college with the understanding that, after two years, I would transfer to a state university and pursue medical school. I had my sights set on being a surgeon.

But at college I was continually confronted with the question "What does God want you to do?" I had never really given the notion much thought. Then passages of Scripture that dealt with preaching and ministry began to stand out during my devotional times. When individuals spoke in chapel on the subject of ministry, something would stir in my heart.

Halfway through my sophomore year, my struggle became more intense. It reached a crisis point one evening when I attended a little church outside of my own denominational background. The pastor spoke on Jonah. His thesis was simple: Jonah was called to preach, but he ran away from God. The message seemed to point straight at my life.

He then invited those who believed God might be calling them into ministry to come forward. I disliked public invitations so I didn't budge. But later that night, I met the pastor in the basement of the church. By then I had made my decision. I said to him, "If the Lord wants me to preach, I'll preach. In fact, whatever he wants me to do, I'll do."

Though the shape and nature of that call has changed over the years, this remains my call: to preach. And when there have been some harrowing storms to weather, the remembrance of this original call is one of the things that has helped me stick to it.

Busting the Four Myths of Ministry

Another tactic when the call to ministry seems in doubt is to remember the four myth-busters of ministry. The first three I heard from Truman Dollar; the last I added from my own experience.

1. It is never as bad as you think it is. Even when things seem darkest, circumstances are usually not as hopeless or awful as they first appear. For example, after one particularly tough committee meeting in which I was left with the impression people didn't trust me, I received a call from my wife.

"You won't believe it, Ed, but you just received a beautiful bouquet of flowers," she said. "Let me read the card to you. 'To Ed Dobson, Pastor of the Year.' "

The flowers had been sent by a couple who had been separated for nearly two years. Through the church's ministry, they had been won to Christ and had decided to be reconciled. I had conducted their marriage renewal service. The flowers were a way of saying thanks.

The bouquet was a dramatic reminder that I should never let church politics or conflicts obscure my vision of the bigger things God may be doing in the church.

2. It's never as good as you think it is. There are times in church ministry when everything seems to be going marvelously. That's when you need to be careful. It's only an illusion. As Jerry Falwell used to say, "In ministry I've never had two good days back to back."

As I mentioned, the letters I shared at the beginning of the chapter were written the same week I was riding high from our tremendous Easter Sunday experience. They were sullen and dramatic reminders that not everyone saw the service as I did.

3. It's never completely fixed. Ministry is a process; it's people. To say, "I've taken care of this problem. It won't recur," is to live in a fool's paradise. Problems can come back to plague you long after you thought they were resolved.

4. It's never completely broken. Not long ago, a pastor from Kenya spoke in our morning worship service. He pointed out that during the first thirty years of missionary efforts in Kenya, more missionaries died than the number of converts who were won. In the remote inland regions of the country, missionaries sometimes arrived with their belongings stored in coffins. They were resigned to the fact that they would never make it back to the coast.

In spite of the difficulties and slowness of progress, these men and women were still convinced that Kenya wasn't completely broken. And so they kept at their callings, knowing that someday their work would bear fruit.

They were right. Thanks to their efforts, today 82 percent of Kenya is at least nominally Christian. Evangelicals alone number nearly 9 million.

Handling Criticism

When I was younger, rather than using my call as a pillar to lean on during times of criticism, I used it as a baseball bat to confront my critics.

Part of that was due to my training. It had been drilled into me during college that regardless of the cost, you have to take a stand. If the whole world is against you, take a stand. So during my first pastorate, I interpreted that to mean I should stand up to my critics.

When I encountered conflict in board meetings, I would bring up the issue in my sermon the next Sunday.

"God called me to start this church," I would remind the congregation. "If you don't like it, there are a number of other churches in this town you can attend." I declared the authority of the pastor and expected that to end the issue.

As I look back, that was stupid. While we ought to stand for what we believe, Paul says we are to teach and admonish others in a spirit of patience and gentleness.

Many pastors don't run aground in ministry because they lack legitimate calls. Rather it's because they haven't been adequately prepared to work with people. They may have been trained to handle the Greek and Hebrew text, but they aren't equipped to deal with imperfect people in an imperfect world. Sometimes, opposition isn't a sign you don't belong in the ministry, it's simply part of the call to "Deny yourself, take up your cross and follow me."

I believe I've grown in this regard. Here are three ways I handle criticism today.

● *Accept it as part of the package.* Some people are attracted to ministry because it seems to be a place of power, influence, and authority. Others think that if they become pastors, "I can read the Bible and pray all day."

Paul was much more realistic in his description of the ministry, and his description is something I need to read from time to time: "We are hard pressed on every side, but not crushed; perplexed, but not in despair; persecuted, but not abandoned; struck down, but not destroyed" (2 Cor. 4:8–9).

The ministry is sometimes pressure, discouragement, disappointment, heartache, criticism, and conflict. I try to communicate that to all who are considering the job. If they don't believe me, I just show them my mail.

● *Don't believe everything you hear.* Recently a woman shook my hand after one service and said, "Good grief, Pastor! Your hand is soft. I bet you haven't seen a good day's work in your entire life."

She grinned, turned, and walked off. She obviously didn't know how such a statement can hit pastors. I just stood there thinking to myself, *Thank you very much. Good day to you as well!*

A lot of criticism people throw our way is based on ignorance or misconceptions. When it's appropriate, I try to educate people. But when it's not, I find it best just to forget the comment.

● *Ask God about it.* When I encounter tough opposition or a stinging criticism, I ask myself, "Is God trying to show me something in this? Is this a process of character development in my own life?"

So I sometimes take these criticisms to the Lord in prayer: "This is what they've said about me Lord. Is it true? Help me to be honest with myself and determine what truth, if any, lies behind their comment."

I will actually read to God the letters critical of me. Sometimes I discover God is trying to say something to me. Other times, he reassures me that I'm on the right track and not to become discouraged.

Listen for God's New Leading

Sometimes when we're doubting the call, we're merely doubting the call to a specific ministry. And sometimes the doubt is justified: God wants us to move on to another ministry.

How we know that, of course, is no simple process. Here are the steps I take to discover if God is leading me to a new ministry.

First, I listen to my journal. I've found that journaling has helped me hear the voice of God for my life. For years, I've taken time to write out, several times a week, what I'm learning from my study of Scripture, my circumstances, and my ministry experiences.

As I was considering Calvary Church in Grand Rapids, I had also been contacted by a church in New York City. New York looked like an attractive option. I would be downtown, in the midst of several million unchurched people.

During that period, I spent a lot of time reviewing my journals. I would notice, for instance, that I would jot down something like, "I'm going to delay Grand Rapids. New York is really where I want to go. Logically, it seems the right place." Then I'd go home that night and get a call from the board chairman in Grand Rapids, inviting me to fly in the next day. Being caught off guard, I would say, "Okay. I think I can do that."

In fact, I noticed that every time I decided to close a door to Grand Rapids, something unusual like this would happen, which would open it up even wider. At the same time, the church in New York would ask me to jump through one more hoop: get another reference, send another sermon, whatever.

As I reviewed my journal, the pattern became obvious, and eventually I followed God's leading to Grand Rapids.

In addition, I think it's appropriate to "lay out the fleece," not in the sense of testing God but only to assure myself that, in fact, God is leading.

For example, before coming to Grand Rapids, I decided I needed to have 95 percent of the congregational vote if I were to come.

"We don't vote unanimously for anything," a board member had warned me. Nonetheless, that was the precentage I needed to feel secure in accepting the call.

I ended up with unanimous calls from the committee and the board and a 99.7 percent vote from the congregation. I've never seen that happen again in this church, even when we have voted on mission candidates or ordaining someone to the ministry.

I've also begun praying with my wife about such decisions. That's not the way the previous generation often went about it. My father operated much more on a priestly model of leadership. God speaks to the priest (the man), and he leads the family, with or without the spouse's consent.

Dad, much to his credit, went from a large church in Ireland "downhill" to smaller and smaller churches. By the time he reached his last church, it had approximately eighty people. While he was always confident of these moves, it usually took my mother approximately a year and a half to adjust to the change.

At the beginning of our life together, Lorna and I agreed that wherever God called me, we would go together. But through the years, I have felt it important to bring her more and more into the decision-making process. I'm grateful I have done that. When the moment of truth arrived regarding PTL or Grand Rapids, she said, "Ed, there's no need to even pray any further about this. Calvary Church is where you belong."

Finally, sometimes we just have to go out on faith, and if we've misread God's will, then that too can lead us to the real calling he has for us.

When I was first starting in ministry, I believed God had called me to become the heir apparent to Billy Graham. I honestly believed I was going to one day take over for him. So right out of college, I set up the Eddy Dobson Evangelistic Association. My wife and I sent out hundreds of letters advertising our availability. If I could summarize the general response, it was, "Paul we know. Jesus we know. But who are you?"

The end result was that we moved into a one-bedroom apartment, and I took a job digging graves. My wife went to work for a temporary employment agency. I was severely disillusioned by the response to what I perceived to be my call.

But this turn of events eventually led to my being offered a position at Liberty College working with Jerry Falwell, and that, in turn, led to my becoming the pastor of a small, mountain church in West Virginia, my first full-time pastoral experience.

When It's Time to Set Aside the Call

Though most of the time the call to ministry is intended for life, there are situations when the call must be set aside, either temporarily or permanently.

● *A breach of trust.* When serious violations of trust occur, involving moral default, dishonesty, or some other significant compromise of personal integrity, it creates a situation where the person, at least for the immediate future, is disqualified from continuing to serve.

Why? Because he can no longer exercise spiritual leadership. That's one of the unique aspects of our calling. A surgeon can be a good surgeon without being a moral individual. A pilot can be a good pilot and lead a reprehensible personal life. But a pastor can't be a good pastor without living a consistent walk of purity and moral integrity.

At the same time, I'm committed to the principle of restoration. It doesn't happen immediately, or without cost. It requires a process of slowly rebuilding integrity and trust. It occurs in progressive fashion, building from one level to the next. Those steps are: restoration to God, restoration to your family, restoration to the community of believers, restoration of the exercise of your spiritual gift, and finally, restoration to leadership.

The first four levels are always possible. But the final level, restoration to leadership, is something left to God and the group of people considering the person for a leadership position.

In recent years, several prominent Christian figures have been restored to their previous ministries. In some cases, they have even gone back to serve in the churches they left following their moral lapse. Still, once trust has been betrayed and your reputation is no longer without reproach, it's difficult to regain the same personal influence you once had.

● *A pause for refreshment.* At any given time, we have sitting in our congregation at least half a dozen pastors recovering from burnout. They are all in various stages of healing. Some just need a place to come and find anonymity. Others need friends and counselors to walk with them through their hurt. They all have one thing in common: ministry has temporarily overwhelmed them.

I always encourage hurting and tired pastors to find the healing and renewal they need inside a church. The first steps are to seek out the leadership of a church, admit your need, and ask to come under the church's care. After a period of healing and renewal, you need this group's affirmation that you're spiritually and emotionally ready to re-enter pastoral ministry.

● *A new calling.* Sometimes God wants a person in pastoral ministry for only one period of life. One man I know was happily serving as a pastor of a congregation in California. He had been writing on the side for a few years, when suddenly one journal he had written for asked him to become an associate editor.

The first time the journal offered the position, he turned it down. He felt he was called to church ministry, and that was that. But when the editor of the journal called six months later with the same offer, he felt a pull to do it. Still he debated: he was happy in ministry, but he thought he could be happy in journalism. Finally what determined his choice was that mysterious inner leading that God sometimes gives us.

Since going into Christian journalism, he has lost his passion to pastor, but he has been given more and more passion to see God's truths communicated in the printed word. A couple of years after the move, he decided to forsake his ordination, partly because he had always believed that ordination implied ministry in the local church, partly because he felt God had opened a new calling for him.

Preventive Medicine

Pastors sometimes are frustrated in their callings because they're waiting for someone to intervene and help them out. They honestly believe that the board will one day approach them and say, "Pastor, you need to take some time off with your family for personal and spiritual renewal."

It won't happen.

Fortunately, I was given this blunt but life-saving advice when I first arrived in Grand Rapids. Our city has a strong Dutch community, so my first year a member of my board met with me on a weekly basis. His goal was to help me understand the Dutch people and the peculiar culture of our church.

"One of the things you need to know, Pastor," he said, "is that we will sit in the board meetings and discuss the tremendous pressures you face, how hard you work, how you are away from your family too much, how you need to slow down, and how important it is you take regular days off and get away for your full vacation each year. Then we'll go home saying to ourselves, 'My, aren't we taking wonderful care of Ed Dobson!' "

Then he leaned forward and said, "The truth is, Pastor, despite our pious lectures and good intentions, we will cheer you right into your grave. We will bury you, and then get someone else to replace you, just as we always have."

He was not being cynical. He was simply warning me that if I didn't take care of my own physical, spiritual, and emotional health, no one else would.

In particular, I need to monitor my physical health and emotional stability. While we may carry the treasure of the gospel with us, we need to remember it's stored in clay vessels. I need to be in touch with the limitations of my clay body.

First, that means proper exercise and diet. I run between three and seven miles a day, for instance, and that leaves me refreshed and pumped up for preaching or teaching, particularly midweek when my energy can lapse.

Furthermore, I know I need a minimum of seven or eight hours of sleep each night to function well. When I traveled with Jerry Falwell, I noticed he rarely needed more than three or four hours of sleep a night. Though he did all the interviews and speaking, I came back from those road trips dead tired. If I tried to keep that same schedule, I'd get sick.

As Bill Hybels has suggested, I also watch my emotional gauges. I work hard to keep my schedule in balance so that I don't go from one emotionally draining situation to another. For example, I sometimes plan golf games between stressful meetings. I also accept the fact that on Mondays I'm drained from the day before. So I don't accept any appointments other than lunch. I read and avoid seeing people or dealing with tough issues. It's a day I use to study and begin preparations for the next Sunday.

Part of emotional monitoring means staying in touch with my spiritual limitations. That means I try and operate primarily in the realm of my giftedness. My limitations are in the area of counseling and administration. As much as my board would love to see me be more assertive in administrative matters, I've told them, "If you want to make me miserable, make me an administrator." They understand my limitations.

Finally, a great way to renew my own sense of calling is to help train others in their callings to ministry. I give to young people materials that will help them sort out whether God is calling them to ministry. I correspond with many seminary students, and I make it a priority to meet with young people who are planning to enter seminary or are home on break from seminary. I also try to give the pulpit to our potential pastors, because I want our high school kids to see this is an option for their lives.

I was struck by a recent interview with Billy Graham in which he said he felt like a failure. I've always admired his simplicity and single focus, so it was disconcerting to hear him express disappointment in himself. He said if he had it to do all over again, he would travel less, study more, and spend more time with his family.

Oh, rats, I thought to myself. *There's no hope for me. Even my greatest hero thinks he has fallen short.*

That was a good reminder. No matter how hard I work at ministry, I will always feel as if there is something more I could or should be doing for God. That is an ongoing frustration of our unique call.

But Billy Graham said one other thing: he believes he did the one thing God called him to do — preach the gospel.

My hope is that forty years from now I can look back and say the same thing.

In the face of a hostile, unfriendly world, we have to spend a lot of our time reacting to what the world does. But we don't have to build high walls and retreat from the action.

— Craig Brian Larson

Epilogue

Recently the Chicago Bears played another of their great games in their rivalry with the Green Bay Packers. It doesn't matter how well or badly either team is doing during the season, when these two teams play, it's all on the line. At this point in the season, they were actually playing for the conference lead; if the Bears won, they would be tied with the Packers for first place.

The Packers' offense piled up incredible numbers against what had been a very good Chicago defense. They marched up and down the field, ending up with 500 yards of total offense. Brett

Favre, the Packer quarterback, set a personal record of passing for over 400 yards (he had never passed for more than 300 yards in any previous game).

At the same time, the Bears' offense, which had been pitiful all year (ranking last in the league), played at their usual dull speed. For the entire game, the Bears' offense could do no better than kick three field goals. Nine measly points.

Yet, the Chicago Bears won — 30 to 17! The Bears' defense scored three touchdowns on turnovers: two interceptions and one fumble were run back for touchdowns. The Bears' defense scored more than either team's offense.

In the pages of this book, the authors have shown us a similar strategy. In the face of a hostile, unfriendly world, we have to spend a lot of our time reacting to what the world does. But we don't have to build high walls and retreat from the action.

Our authors have shown how a strong defense can actually go on offense: Pastors can take the good from the culture of therapy and reject the bad.

Pastors' families can not only survive in the worst of inner-city ghettos but end up feeling sorry for those living in the suburbs!

Pastors can personally carve out time for spiritual disciplines even in a hectic culture. They can deal effectively with the people and issues that cause anger to fester in the church.

They can teach members to speak forth what the Bible declares to be right and wrong. They can encourage churches to reach out in love to homosexuals dying of AIDS, to cities in decay, to government bureaucrats in need.

In sum, our authors have demonstrated what our Lord taught long ago: the gates of hell will not prevail against the church of Jesus Christ, not in this or any culture.